THE CRAZY WORLD OF

?WHAT IF...

© Aladdin Books Ltd 1996
Designed and produced by
Aladdin Books Ltd
28 Percy Street
London W1P 0LD

*This edition first published in 1997
in the United States by*
Copper Beech Books
an imprint of
The Millbrook Press
2 Old New Milford Road
Brookfield, Connecticut 06804

Editor: Jon Richards
Design: David West Children's
Book Design
Designers: Rob Shone, Flick
Killerby, Edward Simkins
Illustrators: Peter Wilks – Simon
Girling and Associates
Tony Kenyon and John Lobban –
B. L. Kearley Ltd

Printed in Italy
All rights reserved

ISBN 0 7613 1007 X

A CIP catalogue record for
this book is available from the
Library of Congress

CONTENTS

THE CRAZY WORLD OF

?WHAT IF...

SPACE

AIRPLANES

THE EARTH

THE HUMAN BODY

GIRAFFES

SHARKS

Steve Parker

Copper Beech Books

Brookfield, Connecticut

WHAT IF THERE WERE NO INTRODUCTION?

Well, you wouldn't be reading this! The Crazy World of *What If...?* looks at things from a very unusual angle, making them exciting and interesting, as well as being packed with facts and fun.

The universe is unimaginably vast. Have you ever wondered what else might be out there? Well, read chapter one, *What If Space...?* which describes how the Universe works, what's above our heads, and how stars are born, live, and die. It looks at how we have taken our first steps into space and who might be out there, waiting for us.

Do you like flying? If so, you'll know what an amazing experience it is. Peek into, around, and behind various aircraft in chapter two, *What If Airplanes...?* to see how and why they work. You can find out about the pioneers of flying, how the jet engine makes its screaming whine, why flying boats were once popular, and what happens if planes fly upside down. How do pilots fly in the dark? Which planes travel to the edge of space?

Take a look at our Earth, from its very beginnings to what it is like today, in chapter three, *What If The Earth...?* Read about how the Earth swirls through space, what's going on deep beneath our feet, and how the wind, waves, and weather work. Learn about how we are damaging our home planet and what we can do to help save the Earth.

How could we see galaxies?

Even without a telescope, you can see a galaxy. The faint streak across the night sky is called the *Milky Way*, which is made up of millions of stars. It's actually our own galaxy. Telescopes reveal millions of other galaxies, or clusters of stars, in space.

Size isn't everything

The universe is everything, including the Earth, the planets, the Sun, the stars, and space. Without telescopes, we couldn't see very far across the universe. With telescopes, we can detect incredibly distant objects. Scientists use these instruments to measure not only how large the universe is, but also how long it has been around.

Why did an eclipse cause fear and terror?

Until people realized what happens during a solar eclipse (see page 11), these events caused panic and alarm. Many thought that angry gods were destroying the world, or that a massive dragon was trying to eat the Sun!

What if telescopes worked without light?

They do. Light rays are just one tiny part of a whole range of rays called the *electromagnetic spectrum*. Stars send out light and other rays, such as X rays and gamma rays, into the spectrum. Radio telescopes with large dishes or long aerial wires and satellites detect the rays, to give us yet more information about space.

Earth

Mercury

Venus

Sun

Mars

Jupiter

Asteroid
belt

Where is space crowded?

In the asteroid belt, between Mars and Jupiter. Asteroids, also called *minor planets*, are big lumps of rock. They vary from about 312 miles (500 km) across to less than 333 feet (100 m). Millions of them make traveling through the asteroid belt very tricky!

WHAT IF SPACE WEREN'T SPACE?

The space between stars, planets, and other objects is not a complete vacuum (totally empty). There's a lot of emptiness, but there are rays and waves such as heat, light, radio waves, and X rays. There's also the odd molecule of hydrogen and other substances, sometimes forming huge clouds, called nebulae, that may be billions of miles across. There are also tiny particles, bits of dust, and pieces of rock called micrometeors, whizzing around. Near the Earth there's debris such as old rockets and satellites, space-station refuse, lost tools, and other waste. They all make spacewalks rather risky!

What's a shooting star?

A famous movie actor with a gun? No, a shooting star is a lump of rock, called a meteor, that rushes through space and travels close to Earth. As it enters our atmosphere and pushes through the air, the friction, or rubbing, against the air molecules, makes it hot. The meteor glows redhot and burns up, creating a flash, or trail of light, known as a shooting star (falling star). A large meteor might not burn up completely, and can crash onto the Earth's surface as a meteorite.

What if there were air in space?

There would be no need for spacesuits since we could breathe. There would be no need for rockets either, since jet or propeller engines can work in the air. Birds could fly through it, too.

How high up is outer space?

Just above the Earth's atmosphere! As you go higher above the Earth's surface, the air gets thinner and thinner. Eventually there is almost nothing left, and you are in outer space. But there's no obvious dividing line. Normal air has all but disappeared by 62 miles (100 km). The top layer of the atmosphere, the exosphere, begins at about 250 miles (400 km) above the ground. Yet the first "space" satellite, Sputnik 1, orbited the Earth as low as 143 miles (230 km).

Could we land on Venus?

Venus is similar in size to the Earth. But its atmosphere has clouds of corrosive sulfuric acid, and the surface temperature is 869°F (465°C). Not the place for a vacation!

Which planet is not named after a god?

All of the planets are named after Roman or Greek gods, except for Earth. It is named after the Old English word, "eorthe," meaning land or soil.

WHAT IF A SPACE PROBE TRIED TO LAND ON SATURN?

It would be very difficult, because there is hardly any "land" to land on! Saturn is the second largest planet, 75,335 miles (120,536 km) across, made up of mainly hydrogen and helium. A space probe would pass the planet's beautiful rings and disappear into the immense gas clouds of the atmosphere. As the probe fell deeper, the pressure would increase, and before long crush the probe. Further down, the pressure is so great that the gases are squeezed into liquid. The planet's core is a small, rocky lump.

The planet of fire and ice

Mercury, the planet closest to the Sun, is only 3,048 miles (4,878 km) in diameter. Its atmosphere has been blasted away by powerful solar winds. This rocky ball has daytime temperatures ranging from over 806°F (430°C) – hot enough to melt lead – to a bone-chilling -292°F (-180°C)!

Stormy weather

Jupiter has a storm three times the size of Earth, about 25,000 miles (40,000 km) across. It's called the Great Red Spot, and drifts around the planet's lower half. A gigantic vortex sucks up corrosive phosphorus and sulfur, in a huge swirling spiral. At the top of this spiral, the chemicals spill out, forming the huge spot, before falling back into the planet's atmosphere.

Are there canals on Mars?

Not really. But there are channels or canyons. In 1877 Italian astronomer Giovanni Schiaparelli described lines crisscrossing the surface of the "Red Planet." He called them canali which means "channels."

What are planetary rings made of?

Saturn has the biggest and best rings – six main ones, made up of hundreds of ringlets. They are 175,000 miles (280,000 km) in diameter – twice the planet's width. They are made from blocks of rocks, ranging from a few inches to about 16 feet (5 m), swirling around the planet, and covered with glistening ice. Jupiter, Neptune, and Uranus also have fine rings.

Which planet is farthest from the Sun?

Pluto. No, Neptune. No – both! On average, Pluto is the outermost planet. This small, cold world is only 1,438 miles (2,300 km) across, with a temperature of -364°F (-220°C). Its orbit is squashed, so for some of the time, it's closer to the Sun than its neighbor Neptune. In fact, Pluto is within Neptune's orbit until 1999.

WHAT IF WE HAD MANY MOONS?

If the Earth had a lot of moons, night creatures might get confused. Moths use the Moon to find their way around – which would they choose if there were more than one? Owls, bats, and other night creatures might not wake up, as reflected light from the many Moons would keep the night sky bright. The Earth would also be more like the other planets. Most planets have lots of moons going around them. We have only one, which we call the Moon. At 2,160 miles (3,476 km) in diameter, it's much larger than most moons of other planets. With all these new moons we'd have to invent new names for them.

Is there a man in the moon?

No, but there were men on the Moon – the Apollo astronauts between 1969-1972. The patterns that we see on the Moon's surface, which resemble a crooked face, are made of giant mountains and massive craters. The craters, which can be as large as 625 miles (1,000 km) across, were made when asteroids and meteorites crashed into the Moon's surface.

The birth of a moon

Some scientists believe the Moon was probably formed at the same time as the Earth, from rocks whirling in space. Others think it was made when a planet crashed into the Earth, throwing up masses of debris, which clumped together to form the Moon. The moons of other planets may have been asteroids captured by the planet's gravity.

Which planet has the most moons?

At the moment Saturn has the most, with 18 moons as well as its colorful rings. This is followed by Jupiter with 16, and then Uranus which has 15. However, as telescopes get bigger and better, more moons may be discovered, so these numbers may change.

What happens if the Moon goes in front of the Sun?

Moon

Area of partial eclipse

Sunlight

Earth

Area of total eclipse

It blocks out the Sun and casts a shadow on Earth, and we get a solar eclipse. But this does not happen all over the world. The total eclipse, with all the Sun hidden, is only in a small area. Around this is the area of partial eclipse, where the Sun appears to be only partly covered.

What's on the far side of the Moon?

The Moon goes around the Earth once every 27 days 8 hours. It also takes 27 days 8 hours to spin on its own axis. So the Moon always shows the same side to us. The far side of the Moon was first seen by the spacecraft Luna 3 in 1959, which sent back photographs of a lifeless moon, with no partying aliens!

Tail

Rocky inner core

Frozen outer core

Coma

Inside a comet
A typical comet has a small center, or core, a few miles across. It's made from pieces of grit, dust, and crystals of frozen gases such as methane, ammonia, carbon dioxide, and water (ice).

WHAT IF COMETS DIDN'T RETURN?

Ancient civilizations thought a comet was a god breathing into the heavens or sending a fireball to destroy the Earth. At regular intervals they would streak across the night sky, creating fear and panic in all who saw them. Comets are really just lumps of ice and rock that boil and fizz as they near the Sun, sending out a huge tail of dust and vapor. In the 1700s it was noticed that some comets kept returning, orbiting the Sun in a stretched-out circle, called a *parabola*. Some just disappear into deep space.

Crash, bang, smash

If a comet hit a planet, there would be a massive explosion. This was seen when the comet Shoemaker-Levy 9 collided with Jupiter in 1994. A series of explosions punched huge holes in the atmosphere, stirring up gases from Jupiter's interior.

How do we know comets will return?

The British astronomer Edmond Halley noticed that the paths of comets observed in 1531 and 1607, and the one he saw in 1682, were all the same – was it the same comet returning each time? He predicted it would return in 1758. It did, and has since been called Halley's comet. From his theories, astronomers were able to plot comets' long orbits around the Sun.

How do we know what's inside a comet?

From observing its orbit and how fast it travels, by studying the light and other waves it gives out, and with space probes and telescopes. In 1986, five space probes passed near Halley's comet, on its regular visit. Europe's Giotto got within 375 miles (600 km) of the core, which is only 10 miles (16 km) long and 5 miles (8 km) wide, and sent back many photographs.

What if a comet didn't have a tail?

For much of its lifetime, it doesn't. As a comet travels close to the Sun and warms, its icy crust boils, throwing out gases that make a glowing outer layer, called the *coma*. The solar wind blows dust and other particles from the coma to form a tail that reflects the Sun's glow, and points away from the Sun. Then the comet heads into space, and the tail disappears.

Largest tail up to 63 million miles (100 million km) long

Tail grows

Comet's orbit

Comet

Sun

Tail shrinks

Tail points away from Sun

How long do comets last?

Some fall to pieces after a few hundred years, while others may last millions of years. It depends partly on how often the comet travels near the Sun. Halley's comet has been seen every 75-76 years for over 2,000 years!

WHAT IF THE SUN WENT OUT?

Who turned off the lights? Why is it suddenly so cold? If the Sun no longer bathed our world in light and warmth, we might last a short time with fires, electric light, and oil or gas heat. But plants could not grow in the dark, and animals would perish from the cold. Soon all life would cease, and our planet would be dark and frozen. In fact this will happen, but not for billions of years. Our Sun is a fairly typical star, and stars do not last forever. They form, grow old, and either fade away or explode in a supernova, a massive explosion.

From the cradle to the grave

Throughout the universe there are massive clouds of gas, called *nebulae*. In some of these, the dust and particles clump together, and over millions of years, these clumps will form stars. Other nebulae are the wispy remains of a *supernova*, a star that has exploded.

What is a red giant?

An enormous human with red clothes? No, it is a star that has been growing and shining for billions of years, and is nearing the end of its life. As it ages, the star swells and its light turns red. Our Sun will do this in millions of years. It will expand to the size of a Red Giant, scorching our planet, before it explodes. Then all that will be left is a tiny white dwarf star that will slowly fade over millions of years.

How could we repair satellites?

If a satellite malfunctions, astronauts can maneuver their spacecraft near it, then float over in a spacesuit with a jet-pack, to make repairs. If spacesuits didn't exist we might have to invent a robot repairman!

Would Alexei Leonov be so famous?

This Russian astronaut became famous on March 18, 1965. He was first to use a spacesuit to leave his spacecraft for a space "walk," floating weightlessly, miles above the Earth.

Could people have landed on the Moon?

Yes, but they wouldn't have been able to walk around. The bootprints of the Apollo astronauts will be in the dust for thousands of years.

Leaky spacesuits

The suit contains a mixture of gases for breathing. It's under pressure, to simulate the Earth's atmosphere. If it squirts away through a leak, the astronaut will be in great danger!

What if spacesuits weren't cooled?

Or warmed, either? In Earth's orbit, the astronaut orbits the planet in about 90 minutes. He would get boiling hot while in the glare of the Sun. As he circled around to the night side, he'd freeze to death! The spacesuit keeps his body temperature within a more comfortable range.

NEAREST STAR
237,000,000,000,000 MILES

WHAT IF WE COULD TRAVEL AT THE SPEED OF LIGHT?

Almost everything in the universe varies from place to place, such as temperature, pressure, gravity, and the size and mass of objects. However, the speed of light is always the same – 186,282 miles per second (299,792 kilometers per second). As you approach the speed of light, strange things happen, according to Albert Einstein's theory of relativity.

What is a light-year?

Is it 365 sunny days? No, it is not a measure of time, but of distance. It's the distance that light travels in one year. Since light travels very fast, a light-year is extremely far – about 5.88 trillion miles (9.46 trillion km) Even so, space is so vast that a light-year is a tiny distance.

Time slows down, and objects get smaller and heavier. Modern science says that no physical matter could travel faster than light, or even at the speed of light. However, radio waves and X rays travel as fast as light, since they are part of the same electromagnetic spectrum.

Space, the final frontier...

In science fiction stories, such as *Star Trek*, characters are always traveling from solar system to solar system in search of adventure. However, even if we could travel at the speed of light, it would still take over four years to reach Proxima Centauri, our nearest star after the Sun. Even then, we would have to find a planet to land on.

NCC-1701

NCC-1701

Could we reach the nearest galaxy?

Not unless science came up with some amazing new theories about travel and going faster than the speed of light. The closest galaxy to our own is the Large Magellanic Cloud (LMC), only 17,000 light-years from home! Other nearby galaxies are the Small Magellanic Cloud (SMC), M31 Andromeda, M32, and M33 Triangulum Spiral. Together they form part of the Local Group of galaxies, in our part of the universe. If we tried to go to another galaxy in a spacecraft like the shuttle, it would take millions of years.

How long would it take to get to a planet?

Mars is probably the best example. It's quite close – it's the nearest planet and also has hard ground to land on, as the Pathfinder has shown. With current spacecraft technology, the latest journey took 7 months. Mars *Pathfinder* landed on the planet's surface in July 1997. It carried a tiny rover, called *Sojourner*.

Can we live in space?

Yes, although the collision between a supply vessel and the solar panels on *Mir* space station have highlighted the dangers of living and working in space. Such crewed space stations play an important role in the space program. Ideas for the future include giant wheel-shaped stations with their own gravity, like towns in space.

31

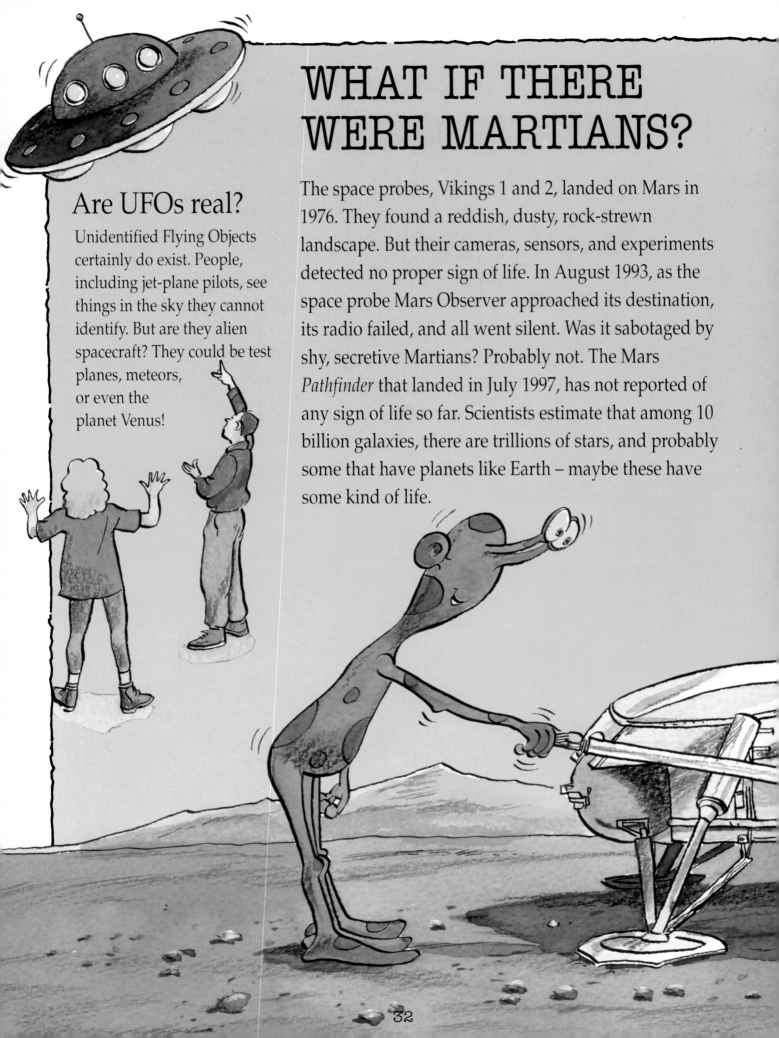

WHAT IF THERE WERE MARTIANS?

Are UFOs real?

Unidentified Flying Objects
certainly do exist. People,
including jet-plane pilots, see
things in the sky they cannot
identify. But are they alien
spacecraft? They could be test
planes, meteors,
or even the
planet Venus!

The space probes, Vikings 1 and 2, landed on Mars in
1976. They found a reddish, dusty, rock-strewn
landscape. But their cameras, sensors, and experiments
detected no proper sign of life. In August 1993, as the
space probe Mars Observer approached its destination,
its radio failed, and all went silent. Was it sabotaged by
shy, secretive Martians? Probably not. The Mars
Pathfinder that landed in July 1997, has not reported of
any sign of life so far. Scientists estimate that among 10
billion galaxies, there are trillions of stars, and probably
some that have planets like Earth – maybe these have
some kind of life.

Are aliens trying to get in touch with us?

Perhaps, but messages in bottles won't work!
Only light, radio, and similar waves travel
through space at great speed. Aliens
might send messages as
coded patterns of waves.
Radio telescopes used for the
National Aeronautics and
Space Administration's
(NASA) Search for
ExtraTerrestrial
Intelligence project
(SETI) have failed to detect such waves.

Are we trying to send messages to aliens?

Yes, we send bursts of
radio messages into space. Also, space probes
carry messages in case they are found by aliens.
Space probes such as Pioneers 10 and 11 have
plaques with drawings of humans, and a
star map showing where we are.

What if they landed?

There's a plan for dealing with
aliens, but it's top secret. Anyway,
aliens advanced enough for space
travel would be much smarter than
we are. So it might not matter
what we did. We just hope they are friendly!

Evidence of alien landings

A few strange cave drawings, paintings, sculptures, and
rock patterns from ancient times, might
suggest that aliens visited Earth long
ago. Some people say that over the
years, aliens have helped us.
But there's no real proof, and
that's what scientists require.

THE CRAZY WORLD OF

AIRPLANES

CONTENTS

WHAT IF AIRCRAFT DIDN'T HAVE WINGS?

Most of them would speed along the runway... and crash at the end, without taking off. Wings make a plane rise into the air, by providing lift. The wing shape also tells you how fast a plane goes. Slower planes, especially gliders, have very long, thin wings that stick out sideways. These wings have a very narrow chord (the distance from the front of the wing – leading edge – to the rear of the wing – trailing edge). This is the same design as the wings of gliding birds, like the albatross. Faster planes have swept-back wings, usually with a bigger chord, like fast hunting birds such as hawks.

An uplifting experience

Some aircraft don't get their lift from wings. It comes from a jet engine or propeller facing straight down, which pushes the aircraft into the air. A strange test craft from the 1950s, called the "Flying Bedstead," did this. So does the Harrier Jump Jet, which can take off straight up, and hover in mid-air. Hovercraft use lifting fans, like propellers facing downward, to create a cushion of air.

What if a plane flew upside down?

First, how does a wing work? Seen end-on, a wing has a special shape, known as the airfoil section. It is more curved on top than below. As the plane flies, air going over the wing has farther to travel than air beneath. This means the air over the top moves faster, which produces low pressure, so the wing is pushed upward – a force known as *lift* – which raises the plane. If a plane flew upside down, the wing would not give any lift. To overcome this, the plane tilts its nose up at a steep angle. Air hitting the wing then pushes it up, keeping the plane in the air.

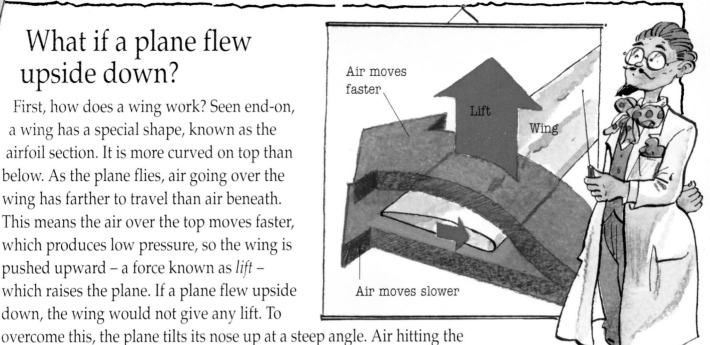

Air moves faster

Lift

Wing

Air moves slower

Can planes fly in space?

A few can, like the X-15 rocket planes of the 1960s and the space shuttles of today. First, they need engine power to blast up there. The X-15 was carried up on a converted B-52 bomber, while today the shuttle uses massive rocket boosters. Once in space, there's no air (or anything else), so wings can't work by providing lift. The power for all maneuvers in space comes from small rocket thrusters.

How do spy planes fly so high?

Spy planes, such as the U-2 and the Blackbird, need to fly high, at 100,000 ft (30,000 m) or higher, so they are beyond detection by enemy planes or radar. However, as air is very thin at such heights, they need very special wing designs, with an extra-curved top surface, to give the greatest possible lift. With the arrival of spy satellites, the use of spy planes declined, until recently. A new generation of pilotless, remote-control spy planes, such as DarkStar, has arrived.

WHAT IF ANIMALS DIDN'T HAVE WINGS?

They couldn't fly, either. Only three groups of animals can fly with complete control. These are insects, birds, and bats. Many other "flying" creatures, such as flying squirrels, are really only gliders, just able to swoop down to the ground. The true fliers beat their wings up and down, to give both lift and forward thrust. Their bodies have many special features. They are lightweight, yet have strong muscles to move their wings. If humans had wings, our chest and shoulder muscles would need to be huge to flap them, and our legs would be tiny to save weight!

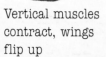
Vertical muscles contract, wings flip up

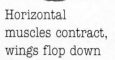
Horizontal muscles contract, wings flop down

Flying insects

In an insect, like a bee, the middle part of the body, or thorax, contains two sets of muscles. The wings are fixed to the outer case of the thorax. As the muscles contract they pull the wings up and down.

Membrane

Going batty!

Bats fly by flapping their arms, which have become long, large wings during millions of years of evolution. A bat's finger bones are extremely long. They support the wing membrane, which is incredibly thin, yet stretchy and strong. The fingers can make the wing twist to change direction, and fold it away after use as an upside-down sleeping bag!

Fingers

Pectoral muscles

Downstroke   Upstroke

How do birds fly?

They go flap-flap-flap! As in bats, the bird's arms have evolved into wings. Very strong muscles in the chest pull the wings down. This pushes air down, and pushes the bird up. The wings and feathers are angled so that some air is pushed backward too, giving the bird forward movement. Smaller muscles pull the wings up. During this upstroke the feathers twist so that air can pass through them, otherwise the bird would just push itself down again!

Thin walls

Cross-struts

What if a bird wanted to save weight?

Natural evolution has already produced lots of weight-saving features. These include thin-walled bones with air spaces for lightness and cross-struts for strength. Feathers also weigh hardly anything, yet they give a bird a streamlined body, a warm coat, and colors for camouflage.

A load of hot air

Birds can stay up for hours by using rising currents of warm air, called thermals. The bird circles around these to rise up, before gliding to another thermal. Glider pilots also use thermals to stay aloft.

Thermal

Human-powered flight

Human legs are strong enough to get the body airborne, with a little help from machinery. The Gossamer Albatross crossed the English Channel between France and England in 1979, using only a human cyclist to keep it in the air.

WHAT IF PLANES DIDN'T HAVE TAILS?

They would be impossible to steer or control! The tail has important parts called stabilizers and control surfaces. The upright stabilizer, or fin, stops the plane from swinging side to side. Attached to the back of the fin is the rudder, for steering left to right. The small, rear stabilizers, or tailplane stop the plane from wobbling up and down. Hinged to their rear are the elevators, for climbing or diving.

Aileron

Controls roll, which is the plane leaning or tilting to the side, for turning, or even spinning right over in a corkscrew-like path.

Rudder
Controls yaw, which is the plane turning left or right.

Elevator
Controls the plane pointing up or down, for climbing higher or diving lower.

Are there planes without tails?

Yes, a few. Stealth planes are designed to be invisible on radar, so they lack an upright stabilizer (fin) because this shows up well on radar.

What if engines were at the back?

Some are! However, you would have to move the tailplane and fin somewhere else. The fin's task might be done by vertilizers (vertical stabilizers) at the ends of the wings. The tailplane's job could be done by small foreplane wings at the front, called *canards*.

How many wings does a plane need?

In the early days, when wing design was just beginning, and engines were not very powerful, many planes, called biplanes, had two sets of wings. The Phillips Multiplane of 1907 had 21 small, thin wings! But it crashed into pieces.

What if planes were like paper darts?

One almost is. Concorde has long, triangular wings along the sides of the fuselage (body), called *delta wings*. These give good lift and stability at high speeds, since Concorde cruises at more than Mach 2 (twice the speed of sound) – 1,320 mph (2,125 km/h).

Swinging wings

Some planes have swing-wings. They are called "variable geometry" combat jets, and they take off and land on a very short runway, such as the deck of an aircraft carrier. The wings swing sideways for take off, slow flight and landing, and then swing back for superfast speed.

WHAT IF PLANES COULD LAND ON WATER?

Many can. In an emergency, the pilot can "ditch" the plane onto water. It's very risky and the plane usually sinks – but at least the crew and passengers have a chance of survival. Seaplanes are different. They are designed to take off and land on water. Instead of wheels, they have long, streamlined floats that slip smoothly over the surface. The flying boat is a type of seaplane with a boat-shaped fuselage (body) that rests in the water. Flying boats were popular when air travel began in the 1930s. Few big cities had airports with long runways, but many were near water. Today, seaplanes are useful in places that have many islands and few landing strips.

Can seaplanes land on land?

Some can. They have wheels that stick out slightly below the floats, so they can touch down on water or land. They are called *amphibious aircraft*. One problem is that floats are quite large, so they make the plane fly slower and use more fuel, compared to wheels which can be retracted.

Skimming above the waves

One of the latest developments for seaplanes is the *ground effect* plane. Developed by Russia, the ground effect plane traps air underneath its wings to create a cushion, on which the plane skims over the waves. A hovercraft uses the same principle.

Which boat has wings?

The hydrofoil is a boat that has ski-like wings on stilts under its hull. As it picks up speed, the wings provide lift in the water (like a plane's wings in the air). This makes the hull rise out of the water. The hydrofoil can then travel at great speed because less of the boat is in contact with the water, skimming across the surface.

How big are seaplanes?

The flying boat Hughes H4 Hercules, nicknamed the Spruce Goose, has the longest wingspan of any airplane, at 327 ft (98 m) – as big as a soccer field. A Boeing 747 Jumbo Jet's wings are 200 ft (60 m) long. The H4 was built in 1947 and flew only once, just 3,000 ft (1,000 m).

Can aircraft land on ships?

Yes. Helicopters can land on a small platform which can be fitted to any reasonably sized ship. Navy ships called aircraft carriers have a long, wide, flat deck for takeoffs and landings by special carrier-borne planes. These shipboard jet fighters include the Sea Harrier Jump Jet, the F-14 Tomcat, and the F-18 Hornet.

WHAT IF THE WRIGHT BROTHERS HAD STUCK TO CYCLING?

Yes, it's true. Wilbur and Orville Wright were really bicycle mechanics! In the late 19th century, the new craze was the "safety cycle." In their hometown of Dayton, Ohio, the Wright brothers set up a business manufacturing and selling bicycles. In 1903, they attached an engine to a glider and produced the *Flyer*. Orville piloted the Flyer on the world's first airplane flight December 17, 1903 at Kitty Hawk, North Carolina.

What if Louis Blériot had taken off late?

He might not have been first to fly the English Channel, on July 25, 1909. He had to fly between dawn and dusk, so the aviator took off from Calais at 4:40 a.m. After traveling 23 miles (37 km), he landed in Dover, England.

On the rocks!

Between June 14 and 15, 1919, British airmen John Alcock and Arthur Brown made the first non-stop flight across the Atlantic Ocean. They flew from Newfoundland, Canada, to Ireland, in a converted Vickers Vimy. In a snowstorm, a fuel gauge became iced over. So Brown climbed out to knock the ice away. A build up of ice could have caused the plane to crash!

How did Charles Lindbergh stay awake?

He had to – he was first to fly solo non-stop across the Atlantic, from New York to Paris, on May 20 to 21, 1927. The trip, in his Ryan Monoplane *Spirit of St. Louis*, was 3,631 miles (5,810 km) and took 33 hours 29 minutes. A former airmail pilot, Lindbergh dozed off several times. He woke as the plane went out of control, diving and spinning toward the waves. But he quickly became alert when he reached Ireland's rocky coast, and flew on to a huge crowd in France.

Do planes get faster and faster?

They certainly do! Since the first powered flight by the Wright brothers, people have tried to fly faster and faster. The Wright Flyer managed about 31 mph (50 km/h) in its short flight at Kitty Hawk. By the 1930s, planes, such as the GB Sportster (above) were zooming through the sky at 296 mph (477 km/h). Since then, the advent of the jet and rocket age has pushed airplanes faster. The fastest airspeed was achieved in a Lockheed SR-71A "Blackbird," flying at 2,193 mph (3,530 km/h) in 1976.

WHAT IF A HELICOPTER HAD NO REAR PROPELLER?

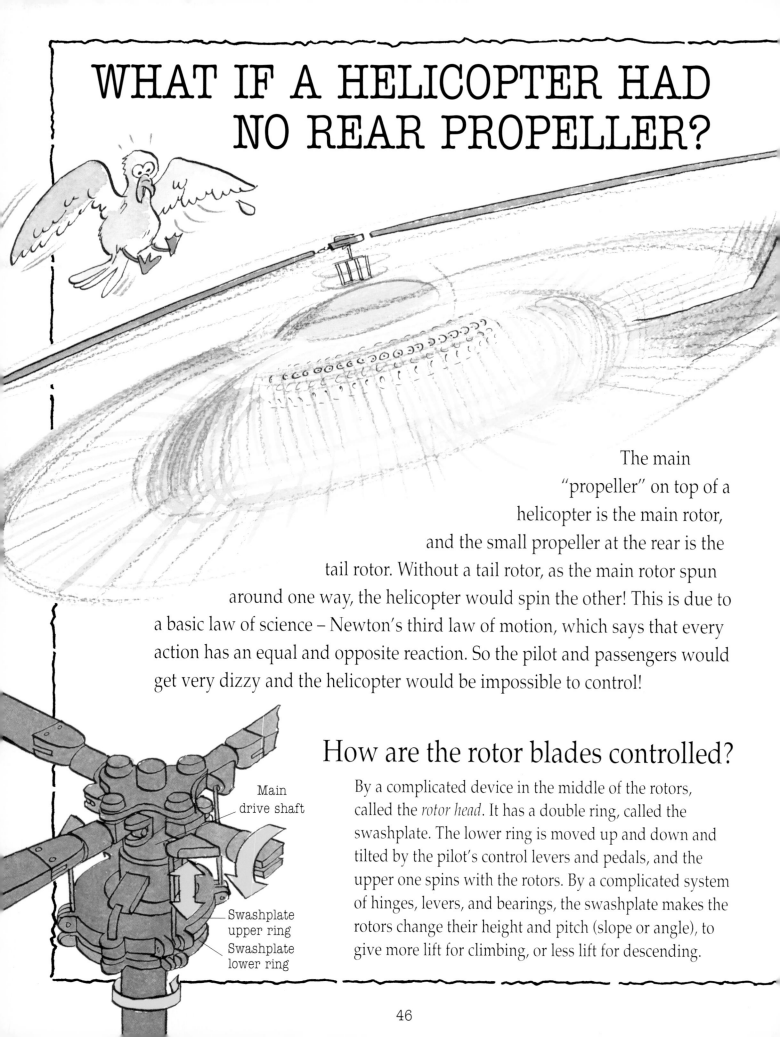

The main "propeller" on top of a helicopter is the main rotor, and the small propeller at the rear is the tail rotor. Without a tail rotor, as the main rotor spun around one way, the helicopter would spin the other! This is due to a basic law of science – Newton's third law of motion, which says that every action has an equal and opposite reaction. So the pilot and passengers would get very dizzy and the helicopter would be impossible to control!

How are the rotor blades controlled?

By a complicated device in the middle of the rotors, called the *rotor head*. It has a double ring, called the swashplate. The lower ring is moved up and down and tilted by the pilot's control levers and pedals, and the upper one spins with the rotors. By a complicated system of hinges, levers, and bearings, the swashplate makes the rotors change their height and pitch (slope or angle), to give more lift for climbing, or less lift for descending.

Main drive shaft

Swashplate upper ring

Swashplate lower ring

What if a helicopter had two main rotors?

Their blades might crash into each other! If the rotors were at slightly different heights, and linked by gears, their blades could always move between each other. This happens on twin-rotor helicopters like the CH-47 Chinook. The rotors go in opposite directions, so there's no need for a tail rotor.

What if a rotor had no engine?

Can a plane fly like a helicopter?

The Bell-Boeing V-22 Osprey can. Its engines and propellers can tilt, so that the Osprey can take off or land vertically and even hover, like a helicopter. The engine then slowly tilts forward so that the Osprey can fly normally.

An autogyro has a normal engine and propeller, and a large helicopter-like rotor that is unpowered. The forward movement makes the rotor swirl around and provide lift, so this craft doesn't need wings.

Is it difficult to fly a helicopter?

For most people, yes. The helicopter is an unstable design, and without the pilot's constant attention, it would spin out of control. Foot pedals control the tail rotor. The cyclic pitch control lever in front tilts the rotors to fly forward, backward, or sideways. The collective pitch control lever at the side alters the rotors to climb or descend. Its engine throttle twist-grip changes engine speed. That's five controls at once!

Cyclic pitch control lever

Collective pitch control lever

Rudder pedals

WHAT IF A PLANE HAD NO ENGINE?

Most planes can glide down in an emergency, like when the engine is falling out. But a plane that's designed to have no engine is a glider, or perhaps a hang glider. These unpowered aircraft sail and soar silently through the air. They always glide downward against the air around them, but they do so very gradually, because of their light weight and excellent aerodynamic shapes. The best gliders travel over 196 ft (60 m) yet descend only 3ft (1 m). The key to gliding is to find air that's moving upward faster than your glider is going downward, such as a thermal (see page 7). A cockpit instrument called the *compensated variometer* shows how fast the air outside is moving up or down, no matter what the vertical speed or maneuvers of the glider itself. Once in this rising air, the glider will circle, and gain height.

How do gliders take off?

In the past, gliders have been launched off cliffs, and catapulted by bungee cords. Some were even towed behind cars. One method used today is the fast-running winch that winds in the tow-rope attached to the glider. Most popular is aero-towing behind a small plane.

Do some pilots hang around all day?

In a hang glider, the pilot hangs below a large V-shaped wing made of flexible material stretched over a metal-tube frame. The pilot steers by shifting his or her body weight to make the aircraft move up, down, or sideways. The world-record distance for a real glider is 913 miles (1,460 km), and for a hang glider, 305 miles (488 km).

Which glider fits in a backpack?

The modern parachute has several sections called *cells* and works partly like a glider. It can be controlled and steered by pulling on cords. Using one of these parachutes, and helped by thermals, a parachutist can stay in the air for 40 minutes.

What if your parachute didn't open?

This hardly ever happens. Parachutes are thoroughly checked and packed very carefully into their bags, so that they open properly every time. However, there is a reserve parachute for use in emergencies, because it is smaller.

Getting heavy!

Big military gliders can carry troops and several tons of equipment, such as large guns and even jeeps. A jumbo-sized glider could even carry jumbo-sized cargo such as elephants! The world's biggest glider is the space shuttle, which comes down to land at 219 mph (350 km/h).

WHAT IF AIRCRAFT PROPELLERS PUSHED AND PULLED?

They do, depending on which way they spin. So it's important to make the engine work only one way, or the plane might shoot backward! A propeller (prop) at the front pulls the plane, while the one at the back pushes it. Both work in the same way, as shown below.

Can propellers work at the back?

Back propellers are known as *pusherprops*. They spin and work in the same way as *pullerprops* (front propellers). They're used in modern microlights and slow-flying survey aircraft. With a pusher-prop, the pilot has a good view and does not get wind and noise from the blades. But aerial control is better with pullerprops.

How do propellers work?

Air pushed backward

Forward thrust

First, each blade has an airfoil section, like a mini-wing. It creates low air pressure in front and higher air pressure behind. This pulls the plane forward.
Secondly, a propeller's long blades are angled. As they rotate, they push air backward and pull themselves forward.

How many blades can a prop have?

The number depends on features such as the size and power of the engine turning it, the design of the whole plane, and how fast you want to go. Many planes have two-bladed props. Multi-bladed props are heavier and need more powerful engines.

What if a propeller was attached to a jet?

It is, sort of. A turbofan is a jet engine with a huge, multi-bladed fan turbine at the front. This blows air at high pressure into the engine, as in a normal jet. It also blows air around the engine, like a prop (see page 52).

Fan turbine

Combustion chamber

How big can propellers be?

Well, their blades must be shorter than the plane's landing gear and wheels, or they would smash into the ground! Also, longer blades mean the tips go faster. If the tip speed reaches the speed of sound, about 763 mph (1,220 km/h), the prop may vibrate and shatter. Larger props must rotate slowly.

Why didn't war pilots shoot off their propellers?

In World War I (1914–1918), fighter planes had just been invented. At first, pilots shot with hand-held pistols or rifles. A machine gun in front of the pilot, where he could see to take aim, would be a good idea – but the bullets might hit the propeller! So in 1915, the designers of the German Fokker fighters invented a levers-and-gears device called the *interrupter*. It made sure the bullets fired between the blades as they whizzed around.

WHAT IF THE JET ENGINE HAD NEVER BEEN INVENTED?

Air travel and air battle would be much slower. The fastest jetliners, and the fastest military fighter and bomber aircraft, are all powered by jet engines. Only jets can move the average airliner along at 563 to 593 mph (900 to 950 km/h), which is nearly the speed of sound. An airliner with the other main type of propulsion, piston (internal combustion) engines turning propellers, could never keep up – no matter how many engines it had! And only jets can accelerate some fighters to more than 1,625 mph (2,600 km/h), like the McDonnell Douglas F-15 Eagle and the Russian MiG-25 Foxbat.

Compressor turbine

Combustion chamber   Thrust

How does a jet engine work?

It uses spinning angled blades called *turbines*, which work like powerful, high-speed fans. The jet engine sucks in air at the front, squeezes and squashes it with the compressor turbines, sprays fuel into it, and burns it in the combustion chamber as a continuous roaring explosion. The hot gases blast out of the back, and thrust the jet engine forward. As the gases leave, they spin the exhaust turbines, which are linked to, and drive, the compressor turbines. Other jets include the ramjet and turbofan (see page 20).

What if the whole engine spun around?

On some planes, it does! It's called a rotary engine and works basically like a car engine, with pistons going up and down inside cylinders. But a rotary engine has its cylinders in a circle, and they spin around and around.

Which were the first propless planes?

The first jet engines were revved up by English engineer Frank Whittle in 1937, but they were firmly fixed to his test bench. The first jet-powered airplane to fly was the German Heinkel He 178 in 1939, with an engine designed by Hans Pabst von Ohain. It was followed by the British Gloster Whittle, in 1941. The first jet aircraft to enter service was the British Gloster Meteor fighter, but the first to get into a fight was the Messerschmitt Me 262, in September 1944.

Silent night

Modern designs of turbofans are much quieter than the earlier turbojets. But many other things affect aircraft noise, such as the height of the plane. If an aircraft can take off very quickly and climb rapidly – Short Take-Off and Landing (STOL) – it soon seems quieter to people on the ground. Many city airports have rules governing noise limits and allow only STOL aircraft.

Could aircraft break the sound barrier?

Without jets, probably not. The fastest propeller-driven aircraft ever flown is the Russian TU-95/142, nicknamed the "Bear." It has been recorded flying at 575 mph (925 km/h) – that's four fifths the speed of sound. Almost, but not quite.

WHAT IF THERE WERE NO PILOT?

Sometimes there isn't. At least, not a human pilot actually operating the controls. Many modern planes have an automatic pilot. It's not a robot sitting in the pilot's seat, but a set of controls incorporated into the main controls. The real pilot sets the plane's speed, height and direction, then switches to automatic, for a break. Of course, if something happens, alarms activate, and the real pilot takes the controls. In very modern planes, the computer-based auto-pilot can even take off and land the aircraft.

How do pilots "fly by wire?"

Computer screens are wired up to show speed, direction, engine conditions, and other information. Small levers and switches activate the flaps, rudder, and other control surfaces. This happens by sending electrical signals along wires to motors. This system is all controlled by the avionics system.

Avionics system

Radar

What is a "black box?"

It's not usually black or box-shaped. It may be bright orange and cylindrical. But it's the usual name for an aircraft's flight data recorder. This device continually records the plane's speed, height, direction, and other information from the instruments, as well as radio signals and voice communications. It is specially made to be fireproof, shockproof, and waterproof. In the event of emergency or disaster, it can be recovered, and its recordings give valuable information about what happened.

Tires, skis, skids, and floats

Airplanes can be equipped with a variety of landing gear, depending on their size and the conditions. Jet liners require wheels to withstand the pressure. Seaplanes need floats to keep them above water. Gliders and early rocket planes use skids, while planes that have to land on snow and ice use skis!

Do you have to be strong to fly a plane?

Not really. Some controls are simple electrical switches and knobs. Others are levers, like the control column and rudder pedals, but they are well-balanced with counterweights and cables, so they aren't too heavy to move. But to fly a plane well, you do have to be alert and physically fit, with good coordination and quick reactions.

When can you see two sets of controls and instruments?

In the "head-up display." There are not really two sets. Part of the main display is reflected or projected upward onto the front windshield or canopy, or into the pilot's special helmet visor. The pilot can look ahead and see outside, and the controls at the same time.

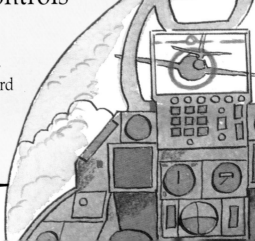

WHAT IF THE PILOT GOT LOST?

Can pilots see in the dark?

They can "see" using radar (RAdio Detection And Ranging). This works like a bat's hearing. It blips out radio signals, and detects the echoes that bounce off other planes or features, and then displays them on a screen. Radar was first used in World War II (1939 – 1945). To keep it secret, there was a rumor that the pilots ate lots of carrots to see in the dark!

A lost pilot could mean big trouble. He or she couldn't stop and ask someone the way. An airplane has a limited amount of fuel, and, sooner or later, it must land. What if the pilot is lost flying over mountains at this time, or thick woodland? What if it becomes foggy, or dark, and the pilot can't find the runway? This is why all pilots must learn about navigation: knowing where you are and where you're going. It can be done by many methods, such as using a compass and radar signals from ground beacons. The pilot can also talk to an air-traffic controller, and use modern satellite navigation, as well as looking out of the window!

Highways in the sky

The skies near busy airports get crowded, so there are flight corridors for planes going in certain directions. Each plane must know where to fly, and the speed and height it must travel – its flight path. The whole system is organized by air-traffic controllers, who speak to all planes by radio and by positional satellites. They make sure that there are no near misses (or should that be near hits?)

Electrical systems

Engine instruments

Airspeed indicator

Engine throttles

Radio and radar

How do pilots tell time?

In a modern jetliner, the time is one of several pieces of important information displayed by the instruments on the flight deck. These include air speed, altitude (height), a compass to show direction, and a radio to stay in touch with the ground control. The displays are on computer screens. A small plane simply has an ordinary clock!

How do pilots talk to people?

Not by shouting loudly! They talk over the plane's radio, mainly to air-traffic controllers in their control towers on the ground, and perhaps to the pilots of other planes, or meteorologists at weather stations. They might also chat to people from the airline about flight times or special passengers, or to the plane manufacturers if the aircraft is behaving strangely. The radio plays a vital role in keeping the pilot informed about what is happening outside the plane.

WHAT IF THERE WERE NO AIRPORTS?

Are there airports in cities?

Not in the very center. A plane taking off couldn't stop at red lights! But there are small airports very close to the city centers. They are used mainly by helicopters, small business jets, and STOL commuter planes (see page 21). Big airliners need very long runways and make too much noise, so their airports are usually several miles away from city centers. There are usually urban highways and public transportation to the city airports.

Landing a huge jetliner in a field would be impossible. It might hit a molehill or sink in the mud. Even if it landed, the passengers would not be pleased to find themselves in the middle of nowhere! Many modern planes need a straight, flat, hard-surfaced runway at least 9,842 ft (3,000 m) long, for safe takeoff and landing. In fact, most airports have two or more runways, facing different directions. This is because it's best for planes to take off or land into the wind. The air blowing at the plane and over the wings creates increased lift for the same speed relative to the ground. This gives quicker lift off and better control on touchdown.

Why can't you stack planes on top of each other?

You can, if you are an air-traffic controller (see page 56). As planes wait to land at a busy airport, they fly in wide circles at certain heights, each several hundred feet above the next. When the runway is clear, the lowest one takes its final approach path and comes in to land. The others move down the stack level, one by one, from the lowest upward.

What if there were no air-traffic control?

At a busy international airport there is a takeoff or landing every 30 seconds. The air-traffic controllers speak by radio to the pilots, telling them which approach paths to follow, where to stack, and which runway to use for takeoff and landing. Otherwise, CRASH! BANG ! SMASH! CRUNCH!

Slam on the brakes

Many planes have brakes on their wheels to stop. Jets may have panels that fold out to deflect their exhaust gases forward. Other planes may use parachutes, or if they are to land on an aircraft carrier, a trailing hook that catches on wires on the deck.

How do planes land in the dark?

The pilot does not use a torch or eat lots of carrots (see page 56). There are landing lights and radio beacons near the airport showing the direction and distance of the runway, and patterns of colored runway lights illuminating the landing area. Many planes have an Instrument Landing System (ILS). It detects radio signals sent from the airport to show if the pilot is landing safely.

WHAT IF THERE WERE NO PLANES?

Life would certainly be different. Airplanes play many vital roles throughout the world, carrying people and cargo to faraway places in only a fraction of the time it takes other forms of transportation. The sky might be full of balloons, slowly weaving about the sky. Instead of crossing the Atlantic in a couple of hours, it would take several days on an ocean liner, or stuck in a small basket under a balloon.

Can saucers fly?

They certainly can. Have you ever thrown a Frisbee and wondered why it can fly? That's because the shape of a Frisbee is similar to a plane's wing. It has an airfoil section which creates a higher pressure below its body than above as it passes through the air, producing lift. It achieves all this without the help of wings. Many planes can achieve the same effect by having their fuselage (body) shaped with an airfoil cross-section. They are known as *lifting bodies* and can fly with only very small wings.

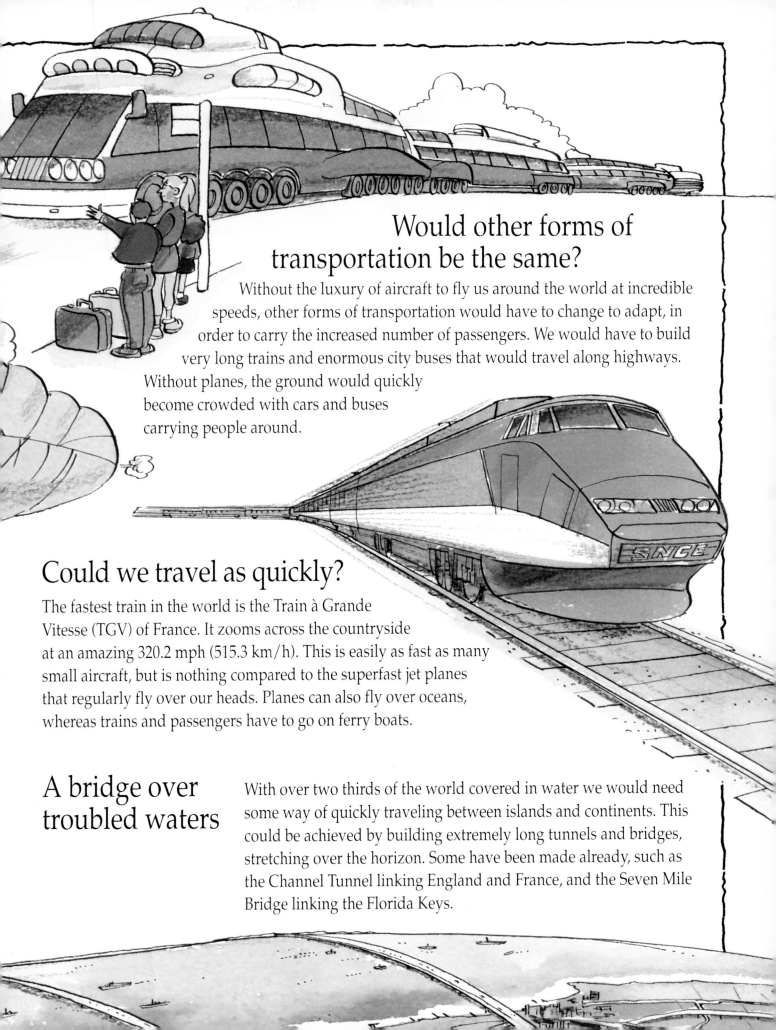

Would other forms of transportation be the same?

Without the luxury of aircraft to fly us around the world at incredible speeds, other forms of transportation would have to change to adapt, in order to carry the increased number of passengers. We would have to build very long trains and enormous city buses that would travel along highways. Without planes, the ground would quickly become crowded with cars and buses carrying people around.

Could we travel as quickly?

The fastest train in the world is the Train à Grande Vitesse (TGV) of France. It zooms across the countryside at an amazing 320.2 mph (515.3 km/h). This is easily as fast as many small aircraft, but is nothing compared to the superfast jet planes that regularly fly over our heads. Planes can also fly over oceans, whereas trains and passengers have to go on ferry boats.

A bridge over troubled waters

With over two thirds of the world covered in water we would need some way of quickly traveling between islands and continents. This could be achieved by building extremely long tunnels and bridges, stretching over the horizon. Some have been made already, such as the Channel Tunnel linking England and France, and the Seven Mile Bridge linking the Florida Keys.

THE CRAZY WORLD OF ?*WHAT IF...*

THE
EARTH

CONTENTS

WHAT IF THE EARTH STOOD STILL?

Direction of Earth's spin

Axis of spin

If it were daytime, the first thing you might notice was that the Sun stopped moving across the sky. You'd wait for evening – but it would never come. It'd be daylight forever! The Earth spins around like a gigantic top on an imaginary line called its axis, that goes through the North and South Poles. It makes one complete turn every 24 hours, giving us the cycle of day and night. As your area of the surface turns, the Sun appears to move across the sky in daytime, and the stars and Moon move across at nighttime.

A still Earth would heat up unbearably on the daytime side.

Daytime on the side facing the Sun

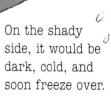

On the shady side, it would be dark, cold, and soon freeze over.

A hard day's night!

If we had endless daytime, the Sun would shine without a break and you might get sunburned. You would also have to go to sleep in bright daylight. People on the other side of the Earth would be in constant cold and darkness. They would become pale and sick.

Keeping hold of the Moon

Without the strong gravitational pull of the Earth which keeps the Moon in its orbit, it might simply float away into space. We would see it getting smaller each night, until it disappeared into space. Then we would have no Moon.

Over the speed limit!

A moving object pushes through the billions of floating molecules (like nitrogen and oxygen) which make up air. The pushing slows the object – this is called *air resistance*. If the air were thinner, there would be fewer molecules, and less air resistance. Objects could go faster, and streamlining would be less important.

Keeping your feet on the ground

With no gravity at all, everything would be weightless, like it is in space. You could float along with no effort, and lift a car or even a huge boat, or train. However, you might float up and away, into the sky, and never be able to get back down again!

WHAT IF THE CONTINENTS DIDN'T MOVE?

The land under your feet may seem solid and still. But each main landmass, or continent, is drifting very slowly across the face of the Earth, by less than 2 inches (5 cm) each year. The Earth's outer "skin," or crust, is made up of 12 giant, curved plates, like a vast, ball-shaped puzzle. They are called *lithospheric* (curved-rock) *plates*. As the plates rub against each other, their edges crack or get pushed deeper. Some plates enlarge, while others shrink. This has been going on since the Earth began, 4.5 billion years ago.

We would see some strange animal meetings!

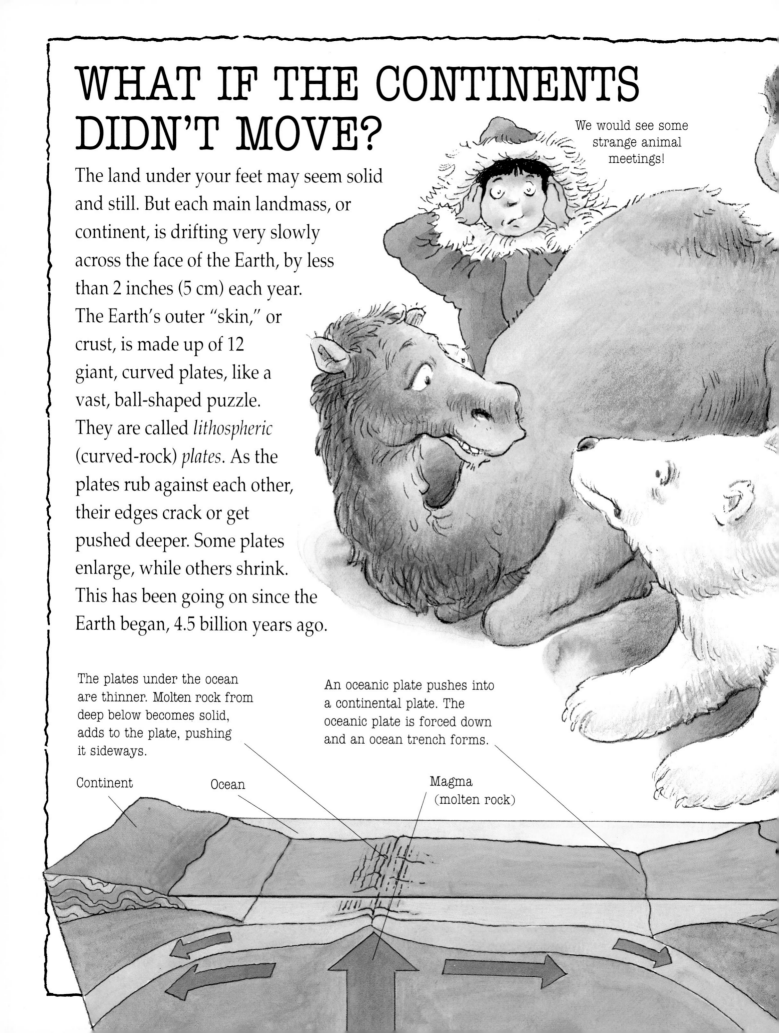

The plates under the ocean are thinner. Molten rock from deep below becomes solid, adds to the plate, pushing it sideways.

An oceanic plate pushes into a continental plate. The oceanic plate is forced down and an ocean trench forms.

Continent

Ocean

Magma (molten rock)

Rock steady

Without continental drift, there could be no metamorphic rocks, like marble. These form when other rocks are squeezed incredibly hard in the roots of new mountains. Igneous rocks, like granite, form when melted rock, such as the lava from volcanoes, cools and solidifies. Sedimentary rocks, such as chalk, form when tiny particles settle in a lake or sea, and get pressed and cemented together.

Pangaea

Metamorphic rock

Igneous rock

Sedimentary rock

Mapping out the world

About 250 million years ago all the continents were joined into one vast land mass, the super-continent of Pangaea. The continuous ocean around it was the Tethys Sea. If continental drift had stopped, the map would still look like this. A journey from North America to Europe, or South America to Africa, could be by car!

The layers of rock in the continental plate are crumpled by movements. This creates huge folds – mountains.

Fold mountains

Highs and lows!

The world would be much flatter and less exciting without continental drift. The deepest part of the oceans, the Marianas Trench in the Pacific, and the highest mountain, Mount Everest in the Himalayas, wouldn't exist.

WHAT IF THERE WERE A LOT MORE VOLCANOES?

The molten rocks of the Earth's middle layer, or mantle, flow around slowly like thick jelly or soft plastic.

You'd have to be careful where you went because a volcano could erupt anywhere, at anytime! Below the Earth's hard outer surface (crust), the rocks are so hot that they are melted. Sometimes the pressure builds up so much that these melted rocks burst through a crack in the crust. This is a volcanic eruption, and the red-hot rock that comes out is known as *lava*.

From volcano to paradise island

Volcanoes that erupt under the sea build up layers of hardened lava, and poke above the water as islands. Coral reefs develop around their shores. Earth movements make the island sink. The coral continues to grow, leaving a ring-shaped reef called an *atoll*.

| Undersea volcano erupts | Hardened lava builds up and coral forms | Island sinks, more coral forms atoll |

Would farmland suffer?

Certainly. Less rain would mean poorer crops, especially those which need lots of moisture, such as rice and potatoes. The lush, grassy pastures grazed by cows and sheep would also dry out. We'd all be affected as food became scarce and expensive. It would take many years to breed new, drought-resistant crops. Camel meat might become very popular!

What would happen to the mountains?

They would not be covered in snow, ice, glaciers, frost, and rushing streams, so the rocks would erode less quickly. Very old mountains, such as the Appalachians, would still be tall, sharp and jagged, instead of lower, smoother, and rounded.

Water, water everywhere, but...

If the water on land ran out we'd have to turn to the seas for drinking water. We can't drink salty seawater, but we can evaporate water vapor from it, to get rid of the salt, using the heat of the Sun or boilers. The water vapor is condensed to make fresh drinking water (like a miniature water cycle). This is called *desalination*, and is done today in hot, dry places, like the Middle East.

Condensed freshwater

Water vapor

Salty water

WHAT IF WE HAD STORMS EVERY DAY?

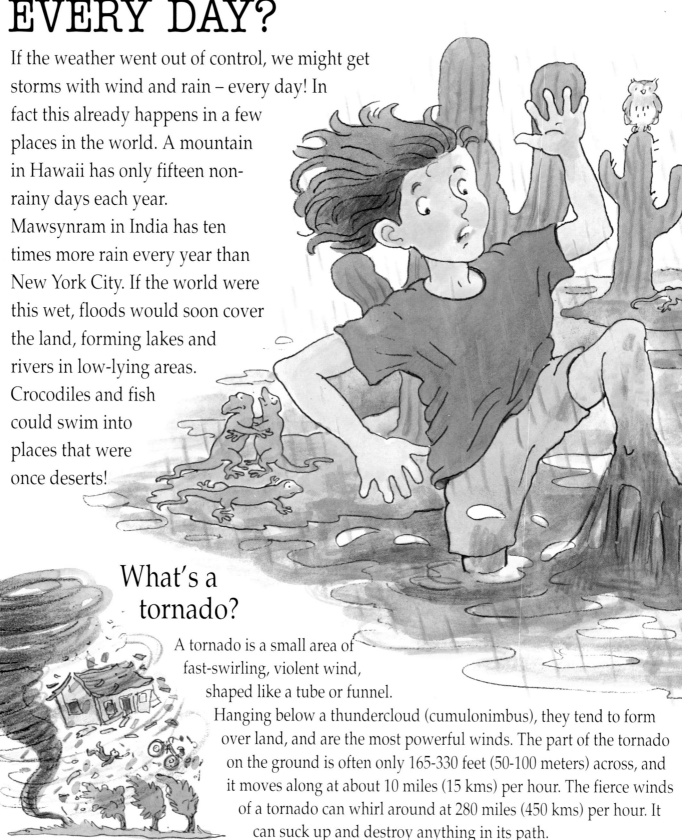

If the weather went out of control, we might get storms with wind and rain – every day! In fact this already happens in a few places in the world. A mountain in Hawaii has only fifteen non-rainy days each year. Mawsynram in India has ten times more rain every year than New York City. If the world were this wet, floods would soon cover the land, forming lakes and rivers in low-lying areas. Crocodiles and fish could swim into places that were once deserts!

What's a tornado?

A tornado is a small area of fast-swirling, violent wind, shaped like a tube or funnel. Hanging below a thundercloud (cumulonimbus), they tend to form over land, and are the most powerful winds. The part of the tornado on the ground is often only 165-330 feet (50-100 meters) across, and it moves along at about 10 miles (15 kms) per hour. The fierce winds of a tornado can whirl around at 280 miles (450 kms) per hour. It can suck up and destroy anything in its path.

What's inside a hurricane?

An area that is warmer, calmer, and clearer than its surroundings! It's called the eye, and it can be about 12.5 miles (20 kms) across. Around it, incredible winds swirl counterclockwise at speeds of at least 75 miles (120 kms) per hour, and often even more. There's heavy rainfall, too – over 8 inches (20 cm) in a few hours. That's as much rain as Oregonians see in four months.

Eye

Strongest winds

Air circulates counterclockwise

Most rain

Positive electrical charge

Negative electrical charge

Would there be more lightning?

Probably. In a storm cloud, fast-moving air swirls around, rubbing tiny, floating water droplets together. This rubbing causes a buildup of electrical charge, or static electricity. When there is too much, the electricity "jumps," as a gigantic spark, to another cloud or to the ground. The intense heat of the spark makes the air around it boil and expand faster than the speed of sound. The spark is a lightning bolt, and the expanding air is a thunder clap.

Lightning bolt

Keep away from isolated tall objects!

Would our homes and buildings change?

Ordinary storms, wind, and floods can damage houses. If we had extra storms, we'd have to change our building designs. A house might have an extra-strong roof that could not blow off, and waterproof doors and windows to keep out the water. Or the house could be on tall stilts, so that the water passed harmlessly underneath, and with a roof that could be repaired easily. There are already houses like this in parts of the world prone to hurricanes, storms, floods, and tidal waves.

WHAT IF THERE WERE NO SOIL?

You wouldn't get scolded for getting your clothes muddy or dirty! But there would be hundreds of problems. Earthworms, moles, ants, and millions of other burrowing creatures would be homeless. Plants could not set down their roots in soil, or take in water, nutrients, and minerals for their growth. We'd have no farm crops, and nothing for farm animals to eat. We'd all starve!

A game of two halves!

Many sports, from football to soccer, are played on soil. Rather, on soil covered with well-mown grass. It's fairly soft and doesn't hurt too much if you fall. Without grass and soil, we'd have to play these sports on astroturf.

Soil soaks up rain like a sponge. Without soil, rain would run into rocky cracks, wearing them into bigger caves and tunnels.

Those feet were made for walking...?

Only a few types of trees can survive without soil. They grow from the thin dust in cracks on rocky mountainsides. Nearly all other trees need soil. The tree's roots anchor it in the soil as well as take in nutrients and water. Without soil, tree animals, like monkeys, would have to walk more, and would get sore feet!

The amazing graze!

Sheep, cows, and many other farm animals eat grass, which grows in soil. Without farm animals, there would be much less meat to buy. Wild animals such as deer also eat grass and leaves. Without them, hunting animals, such as lions and tigers, would run out of food, too. Food chains, and the whole web of life would be unbalanced.

Sweat and soil

If there were no soil, it might be possible for us to make our own. We might grow flowers, fruits, and vegetables in tubs of sand or gravel. But we'd have to keep adding plenty of water and fertilizers containing minerals and nutrients, or the plants would soon shrivel up and die. Natural soil has these nutrients, and does not need a lot of extra care.

Going underground

Rabbits, mice, shrews, foxes, badgers, prairie dogs, and hundreds of other creatures dig their homes in the soil, making tunnels and chambers. Moles live underground almost all their lives, digging through the soil and eating worms, slugs, and other small soil creatures. If the soil ever disappeared, they would need a lot of help to tunnel, as they would be faced with the hard rock beneath!

WHAT IF FOSSIL FUELS RAN OUT?

There are three main groups of fossil fuels: various types of coal and anthracite; gasoline, diesel, and kerosene made from crude oil (petroleum); and natural gas. They are all made from the rotted, fossilized remains of plants and animals which lived millions of years ago. If they ran out, millions of cars, trains, planes, factories, and power stations would come to a standstill. The bad news is that fossil fuels are running out, far faster than they are made by natural processes.

Alternative energy

Fossil fuels can be made into electricity, which is our favorite energy form – efficient and easy to transport along wires. The best ideas for the future are "natural sustainable" forms of energy (below). These don't damage or pollute the environment as much as fossil and nuclear fuels. They will also last because, in one way or another, they're all driven by the Sun's energy.

Nuclear energy is efficient, but it produces dangerous radio-activity that lasts for thousands of years.

Solar (Sun's) energy can be turned into electricity. It is most worthwhile in hot places.

Geothermal energy (heat from deep underground) is easily available in some places, such as hot springs and geysers.

Turbine

Three, two, one... We have lift-off?

No we don't – rocket fuels are mostly made from crude oil (petroleum), so we couldn't launch any more satellites. How about a flying wing covered with solar cells? These convert sunlight into electricity, which is stored in batteries and turns the propellers. Flying far above the clouds, the solar wing could replace satellites.

Reasons for recycling?

To save all kinds of resources. Recycling stops us digging up so much of the Earth for ores and raw materials. It saves the fuels that we use to convert the ores and raw materials into metals, plastics, and other finished products. It stops us from cutting down more trees to make new paper. Recycling is good for the environment. So do it!

A solar car will turn sunlight into electricity for its electric motors. Quiet, clean, non-polluting – great!

Tidal energy harnesses the sea's movements caused by the Moon's gravity. Wave energy comes from wind, but the barrages needed disrupt shore and sea life.

Roadway

Turbine

Hydroelectricity is created by water flowing through turbines, driving generators. Efficient and clean, it can drown valleys.

Wind energy is created as the Sun heats the air. It will last for a long time, but rows of modern wind turbines needed to harness the energy are expensive, noisy, and spoil the countryside.

The holes, or thin parts of the ozone layer, are mainly over the North and South Poles.

WHAT IF
THE OZONE HOLE GETS WORSE?

Ozone is an invisible gas, a form of oxygen. It forms a layer high in our atmosphere, which blocks out harmful ultraviolet (UV) rays from the Sun. Some chemicals that industries put into the air are destroying the ozone layer. If more UV rays get through, they could cause more sunburn, cancers, and skin diseases. We can't sew up the ozone hole, so we must stop releasing these ozone-destroying chemicals, now! In fact, we should take more care of our Earth altogether.

FACTOR 30

How can we kill pests without using pesticides?

Weevils, gall wasps, aphids, locusts, and many other insect pests damage farm crops, as do plant and fungal pests like rusts and mildews. We control them by spraying factory-made chemical pesticides. But these can get into the rivers and soil and may harm wildlife. We should try harder to use natural pest controllers, such as ladybugs that eat aphids, and parasitic wasps that lay their eggs in locusts. However, we must always be very careful. When cane beetles ate the sugar cane crops in north-east Australia, people brought a beetle-eating toad from South America as a natural pest controller. But the toad settled in so successfully, that it has now become a major pest itself.

The global greenhouse

Gases in the atmosphere, such as carbon dioxide, retain just the right amount of heat to enable life to exist on Earth. This is called the *greenhouse effect*. Now we burn more fuels, releasing more carbon dioxide, causing the Earth's temperature to rise. It could melt polar ice caps, raise sea levels, and cause flooding.

Why are rainforests so important?

Because they are home to millions of awesome trees, beautiful flowers, and exciting animals! And they also refresh the air. All plants live by the process of photosynthesis. They catch light energy from the Sun and use it to live and grow. During this process, they take in carbon dioxide from the air, and give out oxygen – the reverse of what we do when we breathe. The forests also affect the weather and global patterns of climate! Burning the great forests upsets the global greenhouse.

Now, some reflected heat is trapped due to greenhouse gases. More heat is trapped

Before, some reflected heat escaped into space.

Some heat is reflected

Sun's rays

Some rays reach surface

THE CRAZY WORLD OF

?WHAT IF...

THE HUMAN BODY

CONTENTS

Hair

Epidermis

Sweat pore

Sweat gland

Dermis

Hair root

Sebaceous gland

Nerve

An average piece of skin is 1/10 inch thick. The upper layer of skin, the epidermis, resists wear by replacing itself. Below is the thicker dermis.

WHAT IF WE HAD NO SKIN?

Skin does so many vital jobs that you'd notice right away if it weren't there. Of course, the body would look dramatically different! Without skin, the fatty and fleshy layers underneath would be exposed. Dust and dirt would stick, and body fluids and salts would leak away. The body surface might become scaly, like a lizard! The body would have no protection against knocks and bumps. It would also be exposed to cold winds or the sun's heat – so you might freeze, or roast!

Don't be thick skinned...

Much thicker skin would protect and insulate you better. But thicker skin has more folds and creases, so we might look like elephants or rhinos! Our skin would also weigh more than usual, so it would be like wearing a very heavy, stiff, cracked leather overcoat, even in bed!

...or thin!

Thin skin might look smooth and sleek, but it would protect the body less against too much heat or cold. And even small bumps could hurt and cause large cuts and bruises.

A skinless body would show layers of muscles, blood vessels, and fat.

Why do we get suntanned?

Skin exposed to lots of sunlight makes more pigment called *melanin*, a dark-brown substance that colors the skin. It shades the skin and parts beneath from UV light and the skin becomes darker. We call this process suntanning. The ultraviolet (UV) rays in sunlight can harm living things. If fair skin is exposed to too much hot sun at once, it will turn red and burn.

Does our skin need its natural oils?

Yes! The skin's mix of natural oils and waxes, called *sebum*, comes from tiny sebaceous glands just under its surface. Sebum may cause pimples, but it is mainly helpful. It makes the skin softer, more supple, and more water-resistant. Otherwise, it would crack like an old boot, and soak up water in the bath like soggy cardboard!

Why does skin look old?

As skin ages, certain fibers in the dermis break down. Skin then loses its stretchy, elastic texture, and lines and wrinkles start to appear.

Hot under the collar!

If you didn't sweat, the body could become very ill with heatstroke! You sweat to lose excess heat in very warm weather, or if your muscles are very active. The skin's three million tiny sweat glands ooze watery sweat (perspiration) onto the surface. As it dries, it draws warmth away from the body. The blood vessels widen too, and lose extra heat, which makes you look red and flushed. Dogs, however, hardly sweat. They lose excess heat through their breath and tongue by panting!

WHAT IF WE HAD NO MUSCLES?

You could not tell anyone that you had no muscles, since you would not be able to talk – or move your head, or your arms or legs. In fact, you could not make any movements at all. Muscles power all body actions and motions, from jumping and lifting heavy weights, to smiling and blinking. These movements include breathing with the chest muscles, and the beating of the heart (by the muscles that make up its walls). So, a body without muscles would be quiet and still, and very soon, lifeless.

Could we be any stronger?

Almost anyone can build up muscle strength, by doing plenty of exercises and by eating nourishing foods. But human muscles have a size limit. Our close cousin, the gorilla, has the same number of muscles as we do, but many of them are naturally much larger and stronger. A large male gorilla is stronger than ten ten-year-old children.

Hundreds of muscles
The body has three main types of muscles. The ones we often think of as muscles are skeletal muscles, shown on the chart above. There are more than 600 skeletal muscles all over the body, making up about two-fifths of the total body weight. The other types are visceral muscles, found internally, as in the stomach and intestines, and the cardiac muscle, found only in the heart.

No orbicularis oculi muscle (eyelids) = no blinking

No orbicularis oris muscle (lips) = no speaking

No intercostal muscles (between ribs) = no breathing

No cardiac muscle (in heart) = no heartbeat

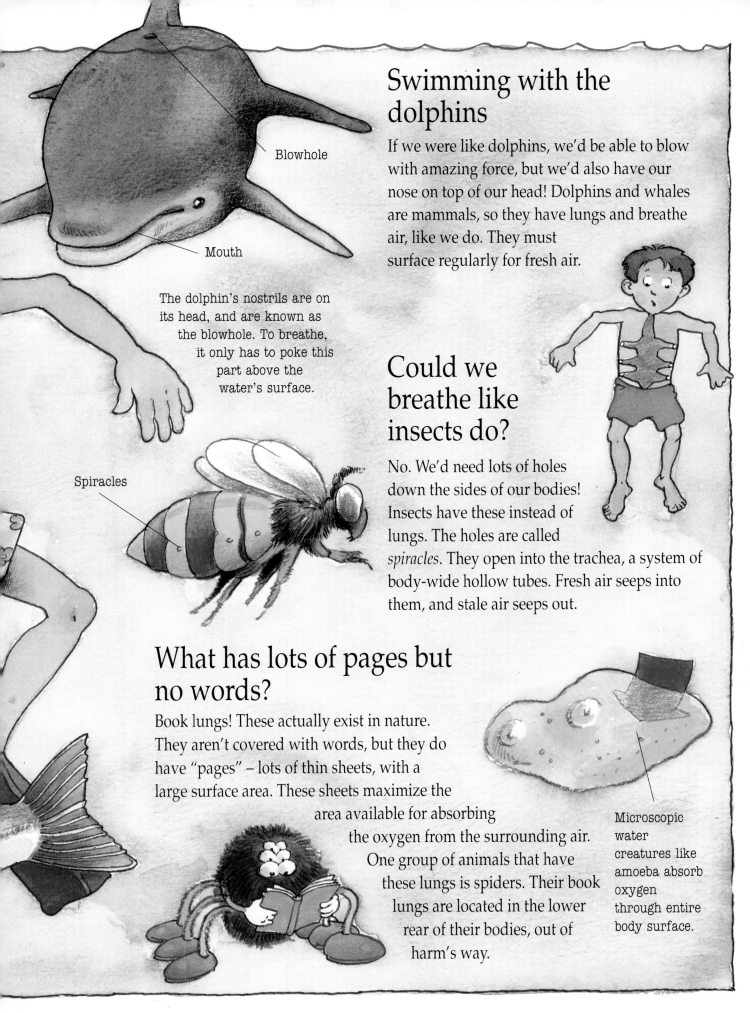

Swimming with the dolphins

If we were like dolphins, we'd be able to blow with amazing force, but we'd also have our nose on top of our head! Dolphins and whales are mammals, so they have lungs and breathe air, like we do. They must surface regularly for fresh air.

Blowhole

Mouth

The dolphin's nostrils are on its head, and are known as the blowhole. To breathe, it only has to poke this part above the water's surface.

Spiracles

Could we breathe like insects do?

No. We'd need lots of holes down the sides of our bodies! Insects have these instead of lungs. The holes are called *spiracles*. They open into the trachea, a system of body-wide hollow tubes. Fresh air seeps into them, and stale air seeps out.

What has lots of pages but no words?

Book lungs! These actually exist in nature. They aren't covered with words, but they do have "pages" – lots of thin sheets, with a large surface area. These sheets maximize the area available for absorbing the oxygen from the surrounding air. One group of animals that have these lungs is spiders. Their book lungs are located in the lower rear of their bodies, out of harm's way.

Microscopic water creatures like amoeba absorb oxygen through entire body surface.

WHAT IF YOUR HEART STOPPED BEATING?

1 Blood into atria (upper chambers)

2 Through valves into ventricles

3 Muscular walls squeeze hard.

You would not be sitting there! If someone's heart stops beating, emergency medical help is needed. Without a beating heart to pump blood through our blood vessels, blood would not flow around the body. So, vital organs would not get their supplies of oxygen and energy-containing nutrients, which the blood carries to them. The brain, in particular, is very sensitive and without oxygen would be damaged in minutes.

Plastic pump
An artificial heart is made of metal and plastic. It is powered by high-pressure air.

What's the value of a valve?

Valves in the heart and main veins let blood move only in the correct direction. Without them blood would slosh back and forth, without direction, and fresh blood could not reach every part of the body.

4 Blood into main blood vessels; new heartbeat begins

Back-pressure closes valve.

Normal pressure opens valve.

Heart

Vessels called arteries carry blood away from heart.

Veins carry blood back to heart.

Does our heart beat as fast as a mouse's?

We'd feel very odd if it did. Our usual heart (pulse) rate is 60-80 beats per minute. A mouse has a heart rate of 500 or more! This is quite natural. Smaller animals have smaller hearts that beat faster, because they use up energy faster. An elephant's heart rate is only 20-25 per minute, and a blue whale's is less than 10!

Blood cells leaking out — Cut

Meshwork of fibers — Platelets

Clot forms — White blood cells eat germs.

Smart clots

If our blood didn't clot, it would keep flowing from a cut for a long time. With a big cut, a lot of blood may be lost and there would be a risk of bleeding to death! Blood clots to seal a wound and help it heal, prevents blood from leaking out, and germs from getting in. Chemicals from the liquid part of blood combine with substances from microscopic blood cells, called *platelets*, to form a network of tiny fibers. These trap more cells, and a sticky clot builds up to seal the leak.

Can blood be green?

If it were you'd probably have two pincers and eyes on stalks, and be a lobster! Not all animals have red blood. In some snails it's blue, and in some worms it's yellow. Your blood's red color is due to the substance hemoglobin in billions of microscopic red blood cells. Oxygen from the lungs sticks to it and gets carried around to all body parts.

Giving blood

If you lost a lot of blood you'd need a blood transfusion. This means receiving fresh blood which is donated in small batches by other people, and kept in cold storage. A healthy human body should contain 8 pints (4-5 liters) of blood.

WHAT IF WE HAD NO NOSE OR MOUTH?

A fly tastes with its feet, and sucks up food with its mouthparts.

Incisors cut food like chisels.

Canine teeth rip food like little spears.

You would not be able to annoy people, by sniffing or talking too much. But you'd be unable to smell lovely scents, or taste delicious foods. In fact, you would be unable to eat or even breathe, since the nose and mouth are the openings for air going into the lungs. The nose is designed to make the incoming air warmer, moister, and cleaner by filtering dust with its hairs. The mouth is designed to bite, chew, and swallow food.

Premolars and molars squash and grind food, like a press or masher.

Bitter

Sour

Salty

A snake smells with its tongue!

False teeth
Some people lose their teeth from decay or injury. The dentist makes dentures – false teeth – that fit over the gums.

A clean sweep!

If we didn't brush our teeth, old food and germs would collect on them and rot, producing acid chemicals. These eat away each tooth's outer covering of tough enamel, and the slightly softer layer below, dentine. The tooth would develop holes, decay, and be very painful!

Crown

Cavity

Enamel

Dentine

Gum

Root

Nerves detect pressure and pain.

Jawbone

The sweet smell of...

If we had no sense of smell, we wouldn't have to smell horrible things, like exhaust fumes, or stagnant water from a polluted pond, or an unwashed person! But think of all the lovely scents we'd miss, like perfumes, flowers, and foods. Also, we might not be able to detect if food has gone bad and smells like rotten meat. Smells like this can tell us important information. A dog has a much better sense of smell than we do, and just by sniffing a place or object, can tell if a particular person has touched it!

A hard act to swallow!

Saliva is the watery substance (spit) made by six small glands around your face. It pours into your mouth as you eat, to make food moist and soft, and easier to chew and swallow. Saliva also contains natural chemicals called *enzymes* that start to digest the food. If you had no saliva, food would be very dry and hard to chew. How would you manage to eat cookies or crackers?

Tongue surface is roughened by small pimple-like projections called papillae.

Sweet

How tasteless?

Without taste buds, ice cream and chips would be tasteless! Flavors are detected by microscopic clusters of cells, called *taste buds*, on your tongue. You have about 8,000 taste buds which detect four main flavors – sweet at the tongue's tip, salty along the front sides, sour along the rear sides, and bitter at the back.

WHAT IF THE BODY HAD NO STOMACH?

The gullet (esophagus) – takes food from mouth to stomach.

Bile in the gall-bladder helps to digest fats.

You'd eat lots of small meals throughout the day, and probably at night, too! The stomach is like a balloon – a stretchy storage bag that expands as it fills up with food and drink from a meal. It squeezes and squirms to squash the food to a pulp, and mixes it with powerful acids and digestive chemicals made in its own lining. The result is a semi-digested soup that, over several hours, trickles into the intestines. Here the food is digested completely into nutrients. These are absorbed into the body for energy, growth, repair, and maintenance.

Monkey business

If you ate like the proboscis monkey you'd have a huge belly, which might make up half your whole body weight! This monkey only eats leaves such as mangrove leaves that are not very nutritious, so it has to eat so much that its stomach is jammed full.

The liver processes the nutrients from digestion, stores some for later, and makes bile fluid.

A full stomach holds more than one-half gallon of food and liquid. Its wall muscles make regular, strong motions.

The small intestine completes food digestion, absorbing nutrients into the blood flowing through its walls.

What if you had no kidneys?

You might save a few minutes by not going to the toilet. However, the kidneys are essential as they filter wastes and unwanted substances from the blood, and form them into watery urine. The bladder stores this urine until you have a convenient moment to get rid of it by urinating. If the kidneys were not there to do their job, the waste substances would build up in the blood. Within a few hours, they would poison the body.

Right kidney

Left kidney

Bladder

Pipe to outside (urethra)

The spleen stores nutrients and disease-fighting white cells, and recycles parts of the blood.

The pancreas makes juices called *enzymes* which attack the food.

WATER

Our water cycle

During digestion, lots of water is added to food, as digestive juices like acids and enzymes. The large intestine takes back most of it into the blood. Otherwise, you'd have to drink ten times as much!

Gone with the wind!

Digestion is a busy chemical process. Like other types of chemistry, it makes gases. These bubble throughout the stomach and intestines and eventually come out of your mouth or other end. It's very natural, but you can control when the gases come out, and whether they make a noise.

The large intestine absorbs water and minerals from the undigested foods, and stores the remains as feces.

Straightening out your intestines

If your intestines were uncoiled, you would be about 33 ft (10m) tall, and incredibly thin! The small intestine is up to 23 ft (7m) long and the large intestine is about 5 ft (1.5m) long. The human body has them coiled up inside the abdomen.

WHAT IF WE ATE ONLY LETTUCE?

Human bodies have evolved over millions of years. They are designed to eat natural and varied foods, especially leaves, fruits, vegetables, nuts, and similar plant foods, and some meats. In the busy modern world, we may eat only a few types of foods, which have been prepared, precooked, and prepacked to save us time. This can be unhealthy. A wide variety of different foods supplies the body with the nutrients it needs. So too much of any food, even lettuce, can cause illness. Over-eating makes us overweight, more prone to heart and blood vessel diseases, joint aches, and other problems.

Sleeping beauty

Without sleep you would only last a couple of days before you started to get headaches, dizziness, sickness, confusion, and other problems. We all need regular rest and sleep, from 20 hours a day for a tiny new baby, to 7-8 hours for most adults. The most important fact is to be aware of the warning signs, and get as much sleep as you need.

Baring all!

If the weather were very warm, it might not matter to the body if we didn't wear clothes, but it might matter to other people! Anyway, if it's cold, you need clothes to keep you from shivering. Humans don't have thick fur like most mammals. So the body could not keep up its natural temperature. It would gradually suffer from hypothermia, and die.

No smoking

The tars in tobacco smoke clog up the lungs and cause breathing problems and diseases. Smoking is also linked to cancers of the mouth, throat and lungs. These can be deadly.

Snails can't see detailed images, only shadows.

What's it like to be eagle-eyed?

The closest we can get to this kind of eyesight is to use binoculars! With our own eyes we can't see faraway things in incredible detail, like an eagle. This hunting bird could spot a rabbit 3 miles (5km) away, whereas you would be lucky to notice it at 0.6 mile (1km). But the eagle may not have such a good general view of the surroundings to see details across its whole area of vision, as we do.

5 The retina, a thin sheet of 130 million light-sensitive cells (rods and cones), changes light rays into nerve signals.

6 The nerve signals flash from the retina into the optic nerve, and then to the brain for sorting and analysis.

Cat's eyes

No animal can see in total darkness. But a cat's eyes are very sensitive to dim light, so they can see about five times better in the dark than we can. The normally slitlike pupil opens very wide, to let in as much light as possible. Also, a mirrorlike layer behind the retina, the tapetum, reflects light. This gives the retina two chances at detecting the rays. And it's why a cat's eyes shine in the dark!

Rod

Cone

WHAT IF WE COULD HEAR LIKE A BAT?

At nighttime, we would hear lots of squeaks. These are the noises made by other bats finding their way in the dark, using sound pulses and the pattern of returning echoes – *echolocation*, or sonar. We cannot normally hear the bat's sounds as they are ultrasonic (too high-pitched for our ears to detect).

Cochlear nerve (hearing signals)

Vestibular nerve (balance signals)

The semi-circular canals help with balance.

2 Sound waves go along the ear canal and hit the flexible eardrum at the end, making it vibrate.

Eardrum

Anvil

Stirrup

Hammer

3 Vibrations pass from the eardrum along a set of three tiny bones, the hammer, anvil, and stirrup, to the cochlea.

4 Vibrations pass into the cochlea, shake tiny hairs, and send nerve signals to the brain.

Eustachian air tube

Can we hear as well as an owl?

Each animal's hearing is adapted to its lifestyle. For instance, the owl's ears are low on the sides of its head, hidden by feathers. They are incredibly sensitive to tiny sounds in the quiet of night. The owl can pinpoint the position of a mouse on the ground, as it swoops in for the kill.

1 Sound waves are vibrations of molecules in air. These vibrations spread out like ripples on a pond.

Keeping an ear to the ground!

Human ears are located on the head with the other main sense organs – the eyes, nose, and tongue. Some insects have eardrum-type flaps for hearing, on other parts of their bodies. For example, the grasshopper listens to its neighbors chirping with ears which are on its knees!

The only way is up!

You know which way is up or down, partly due to your sense of balance. The chambers and semi-circular canals deep inside your ears are filled with fluid and sensitive cells with micro-hairs in them. These detect gravity and any head movements. So you usually know which direction you are moving in, and how fast you are moving.

Your eyes can also see the ground below, the sky above, and upright walls, doors, and trees. All this helps you to keep your balance, otherwise you might wobble and fall over.

Ear-ear!

Many animals lack ears, such as the billions of worms in the soil and starfish in the seas, yet they survive very well! Worms cannot hear airborne sound waves, but they can sense vibrations in the ground. Water animals, like starfish, do not need to detect airborne sound waves, either. However, many have sensory parts to detect vibrations, ripples, and currents in the water.

WHAT IF PEOPLE DIDN'T HAVE SEX?

The human species would soon die out! If an alien space creature came to Earth, it would notice that there are two main kinds, or sexes, of human body – male and female. This is the same as in most other animals, from whales to fish, and eagles to ants. The male and the female mate together (have sex) to reproduce (make babies). A few animals, especially simple microscopic ones, can reproduce without mating. They divide into two offspring (right). This is asexual reproduction.

Animal magnetism

In some animals, such as frogs or fish, the males and females seem the same, but only to us. The animals themselves can tell the sexes apart. Sometimes it's by behavior – the male or female does a courting dance or takes up a certain body posture. It may be the different mating calls and songs they sing, or even the scents and smells they give off which show a difference.

The male body
An average adult male is taller, stronger, and hairier than a female. He has broad shoulders, narrow hips, a deeper voice, and facial hair. But there are many variations.

The male parts

Sperm tube

Sperm

Testis

Scrotum

Penis

The male sexual organs are outside the main body, between the legs. The testes make millions of microscopic, tadpole-shaped cells called *sperm cells*.

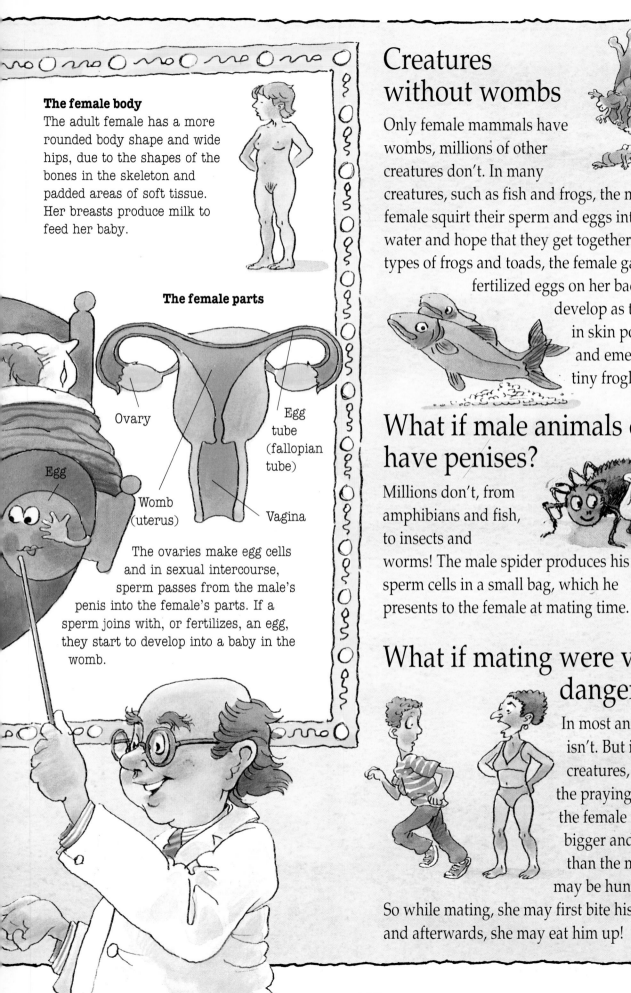

The female body

The adult female has a more rounded body shape and wide hips, due to the shapes of the bones in the skeleton and padded areas of soft tissue. Her breasts produce milk to feed her baby.

The female parts

Ovary

Egg tube (fallopian tube)

Egg

Womb (uterus)

Vagina

The ovaries make egg cells and in sexual intercourse, sperm passes from the male's penis into the female's parts. If a sperm joins with, or fertilizes, an egg, they start to develop into a baby in the womb.

Creatures without wombs

Only female mammals have wombs, millions of other creatures don't. In many creatures, such as fish and frogs, the male and female squirt their sperm and eggs into the water and hope that they get together. In some types of frogs and toads, the female gathers the fertilized eggs on her back. They develop as tadpoles in skin pockets, and emerge as tiny froglets!

What if male animals didn't have penises?

Millions don't, from amphibians and fish, to insects and worms! The male spider produces his sperm cells in a small bag, which he presents to the female at mating time.

What if mating were very dangerous?

In most animals, it isn't. But in some creatures, such as the praying mantis, the female is much bigger and stronger than the male. She may be hungrier, too. So while mating, she may first bite his head off and afterwards, she may eat him up!

WHAT IF WE GREW AS FAST AS A WHALE?

Sperm
and egg
0 months

Baby at
1½ months

Baby at
2½ months

Baby at
6½ months

Instead of taking nine months to grow inside our mother's womb, we would only take a day! In the two months before it is born, a human baby grows by about 4.4 lb (2kg) in weight. In the same time, a baby blue whale in its mother's womb grows by 2 tons – one thousand times as much! The time when the baby grows in the womb is called *pregnancy*.

Most of the development of body parts and organs in the human baby happen early, in the first two months of pregnancy, when the body of the baby is still only 1 in (25mm) long.

Baby after nine months in the womb, ready to be born

The ever-changing human body

Some parts of the human body never stop growing. Your hair, fingernails, and toenails grow throughout life, although some of the hairs may fall out in later years. You have to trim or cut your hair and nails so they don't get too long or dirty. Your skin also grows all the time, since about 13 lb (5kg) of it is rubbed away each year by daily activity.

What happens as we grow up?

Loads of exciting things! You learn to laugh, cry, smile, move about, hold things, crawl, stand, walk, talk, draw, read, write, play games, and study English, math, science, and history. Of course, people are different. Some are good at certain things, like sports. Others aren't. As you grow up, you also learn about rules and laws, how to behave properly and stay out of trouble, how to eat healthily and keep clean, and how to make lots of friends – but hopefully no enemies. Many people find a partner and have their own children. Many get jobs. Older people might take it easy, or stay busy and active! Everyone has occasional problems and heartaches along the way. It's all part of growing up.

How long can we live?

The average age people reach in most western countries is around 70-80 years. Overall, women live about 3-5 years longer than men. There are very few people over one hundred. But how much living you do, and how much you pack into those years, is up to you. Humans live a long time, compared to most animals. Some insects like small flies have hatched, grown, mated, and died within twenty days. Yet some huge reptiles, like giant tortoises, may live to be over 120 years old.

A kangaroo is born early. It does most of its growth not in its mother's womb, but in her pouch.

115

THE BODY SYSTEMS

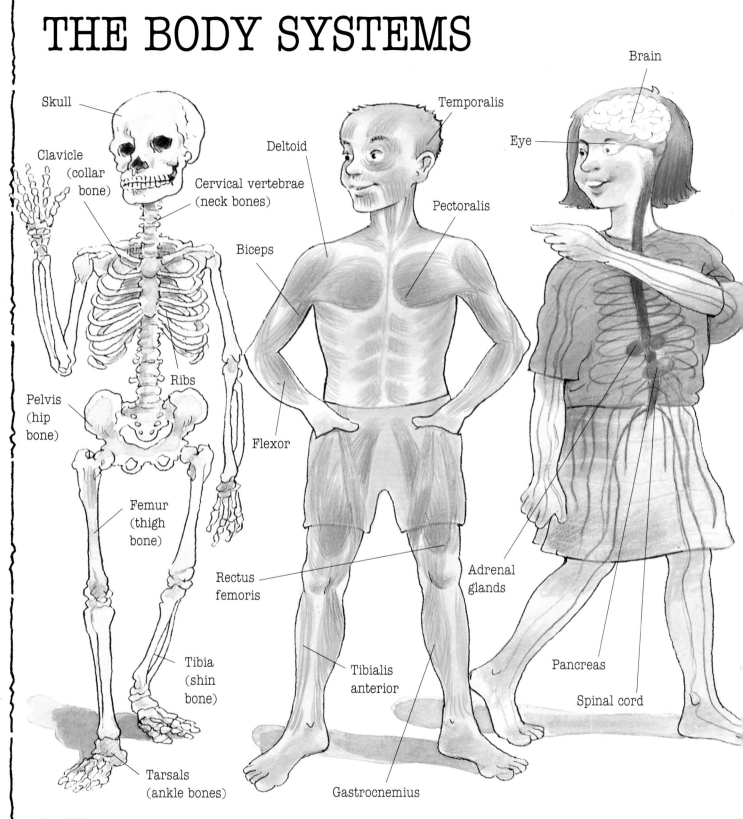

Skull

Clavicle (collar bone)

Cervical vertebrae (neck bones)

Biceps

Ribs

Pelvis (hip bone)

Flexor

Femur (thigh bone)

Rectus femoris

Tibia (shin bone)

Tarsals (ankle bones)

Temporalis

Deltoid

Pectoralis

Tibialis anterior

Gastrocnemius

Adrenal glands

Brain

Eye

Pancreas

Spinal cord

The Skeleton
206 bones provide a rigid framework moved by muscles and protect soft parts like the brain.

Muscles
Over 640 muscles pull bones, so you can move. Muscles are two-fifths of our total body weight.

Nerves, Senses, and Glands
The nerves and glands control the body's systems, using either chemical or electrical messages.

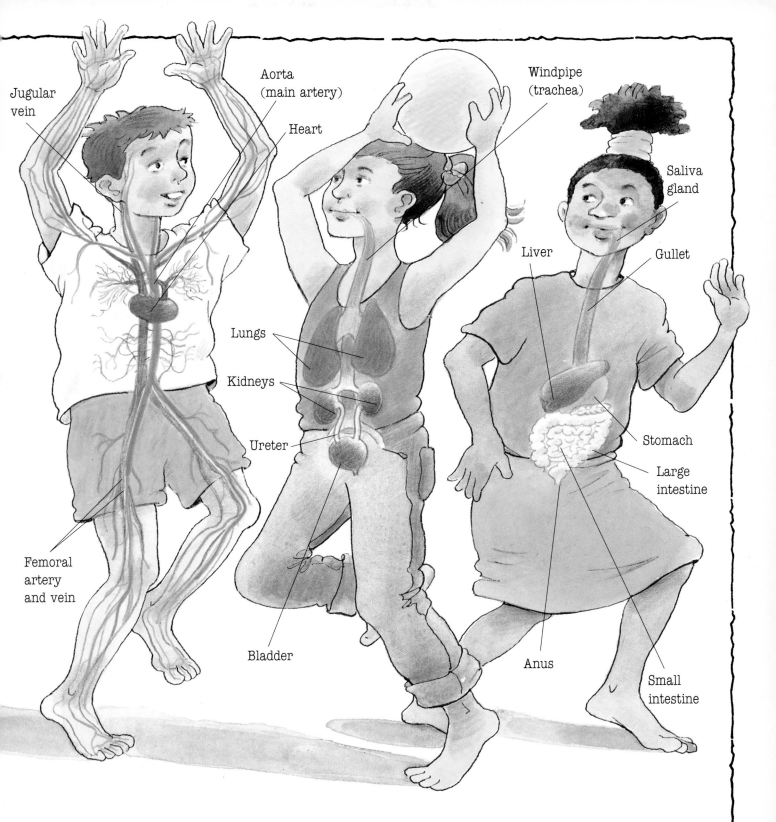

Jugular vein

Aorta (main artery)

Heart

Windpipe (trachea)

Saliva gland

Liver

Gullet

Lungs

Kidneys

Ureter

Stomach

Large intestine

Femoral artery and vein

Bladder

Anus

Small intestine

Circulation
The body's cardiovascular system circulates blood through the blood vessels pumped by the heart. The blood spreads oxygen and nutrients, and collects any of the body's waste products.

Respiration and excretion
In respiration, the lungs absorb oxygen from the air, and excrete, or get rid of, carbon dioxide. The kidneys excrete wastes by filtering them from the blood, to form urine.

Digestion
The mouth, gullet, stomach, and intestines break down food and absorb nutrients into the body. The pancreas makes digestive juices, and the liver processes and stores nutrients.

THE CRAZY WORLD OF

GIRAFFES

CONTENTS

WHAT IF GIRAFFES HAD SHORT NECKS?

Some do! The okapi is a type of giraffe found in the tropical rain forests of central Africa. Unlike its taller relative, the giraffe of the African plains, all of its food is within easy reach among the lush jungle vegetation. As a result, it does not need the long neck of the plains giraffe. The tree branches of the African plains are found well above the ground, so the giraffe needs a long neck to stretch up and eat the leaves that can be over 19 ft (6 m) high. The giraffe's unique feature has evolved over years of evolution, so that it is now perfectly suited to its way of life.

Designed by committee

The odd shape of the giraffe, with its big head, long neck, long front legs, and short back legs, has often been described as an animal put together by a committee. However, the peculiar body has evolved naturally over time. The result may look odd, but it works.

Lookout post

Not only does the giraffe's tall neck allow it to reach the highest branches, it lets it see over long distances. High above the grassy plains, the giraffe can spot danger, such as a bush fire or a prowling hunter, or even new trees to eat, from several miles away.

Okapi

All creatures great and small

Just as the neck of the giraffe has developed over millions of years, so nature has created a whole host of different mammals. There are currently over 4,000 species of mammal, ranging from enormous whales to tiny mice, and from peaceful cows to aggressive tigers. Each of these has developed its own method of survival, involving a bizarre array of physical features. These include the hump of a camel, the stripes of a zebra, or the trunk of an elephant. All of these strange-looking features have evolved to help the animal survive in its environment.

The long and short of it
A giraffe, like all other mammals, including the okapi, has only seven vertebrae in its neck. However, these neck bones are greatly elongated (stretched), allowing the giraffe's head to stand way above the ground.

Giraffe

What if dinosaurs were still alive?

Then we would not be here! Mammals and dinosaurs first appeared at the same time, about 200 million years ago. However, it was the dinosaurs who were first to develop and rule the Earth. Mammals could not compete, and they had to be very small to survive. Then, mysteriously, the dinosaurs died out about 65 million years ago, and mammals were able to develop into their many and various forms (see above). If the dinosaurs were still here, then the largest mammal would probably be about the size of a cat.

WHAT IF A LEOPARD COULD CHANGE ITS SPOTS?

A leopard's spots are designed to break up its outline and keep it hidden, especially when it's crawling through the long grass, or lying on a tree branch. Many mammals have this type of camouflage – both the hunted and the hunters, including tigers. If these animals were brightly colored, or if they had strange patterns on their fur, they would stand out, and enemies could spot them at once!

Dappled deer

Adult red deer tend to graze in open areas. But baby red deer, called fawns, hide by lying still among ferns or heather, under a bush, or in a thicket. The sunlight shining through the leaves creates light and shadow below. So the fawn's coat has similar light and dark patches to conceal it in the dappled sunlight.

What if a polar bear had no fur coat?

Its naked, pinkish body would show up clearly against the white background of snow and ice. So the polar bear would have trouble trying to sneak up on seals to eat, and it would get very hungry. It would also be extremely cold. This is another job of a mammal's hairy coat – to protect against the cold (or heat, as in the case of a camel). The polar bear's fur coat is extremely thick and warm, as well as extra white. Without it, the bear would quickly freeze to death.

Stop blubbering!

All mammals have a layer of a soft, fatty substance just under the skin, covering the muscles and other inner parts. When this is very thick, it's called *blubber*. It makes the seal's body smooth and sleek, and acts as a store of energy should food ever get scarce.

However, its major role is as a wraparound blanket of fat to help the fur keep out the cold, especially when the animal is swimming in the icy seawater. Some seals can have a layer blubber that is more than 4 in (10 cm) thick.

Fur
Skin
Blubber
Muscle

Skinny seal
A blubberless seal would not only look very thin, it would very quickly freeze to death in the cold seas that it swims through.

What if mammals had spears and armor?

Some do – the porcupine has spines and the armadillo has armor-plating. The porcupine has normal mammal fur and also very thick, sharp-tipped, spearlike hairs growing from the skin. These are quills which are only attached loosely to the skin. The porcupine can flick its tail and throw off the quills into an unwary attacker's face.

The armadillo has a covering of small bone plates embedded in horny skin, with patches of tough skin and hairs between them. The plates hang down over the creature's head, sides, legs, and tail. When threatened, the armadillo can roll up into an armor-plated ball.

WHAT IF A BAT COULDN'T HEAR?

Clicks

Echoes

Bat sonar
The bat's sound pulses are so high-pitched that you or I couldn't hear them. However, a bat's hearing is so sensitive, it can hear these clicks and their echoes. The bat can find its way and catch its flying food even in complete darkness. The system is like radar, but with sound waves instead of radio waves. It's known as sonar or echolocation.

It would fly through the dark night – and crash into things! Mammals possess an amazing array of senses to detect the outside world. Hearing is only one of these. They are able to see in very poor light, smell the very faintest odors, taste an enormous variety of different foods, and detect touches and vibrations that are as light as a feather.

Dolphin sonar
Predatory members of the whale group, such as dolphins and killer whales, have a sonar system like the bat's (above). The sound pulses are concentrated, or focused, into a beam by a large lump in the forehead, the melon.

melon

What if whales could sing?
All whales make underwater sounds, varying from shrill clicks and squeaks and squawks, to haunting low moans and groans. Beluga and humpback whales are so noisy that their calls can be heard underwater more than 125 miles (200 km) away. The "songs" of a whale can last between 6 and 35 minutes, and are used by the whales to communicate with each other.

Nighttime eye-shine

If you've ever shone a flashlight into a cat's eyes, you will have seen that they appeared to glow in the dark. A cat's eye has a mirrorlike layer inside, the tapetum. Light rays come into the eye and some are detected by the light-sensitive layer, the retina. Others pass through the retina, bounce off the tapetum, and get sensed by the retina on the way out. This gives the eye two chances to detect light rays. Other nocturnal (nighttime) animals, such as opossums, have this too.

The pupil opens wider in dark conditions, to let in more light.

The retina detects light and turns it into nerve signals, which go to the brain.

The tapetum is a layer behind the retina. It reflects the light back onto the retina.

What if a lion had eyes on the side of its head?

It would leap at its prey, and probably miss! Most hunters, such as seals, cats, and foxes, have two forward-facing eyes at the front of the head. This gives them overlapping fields of vision (right), and allows them to judge distances well, for pursuit and pounce. Most hunted mammals, such as deer, zebras, and rabbits, have eyes on the sides of their head. Although this means that they can't judge distances well, it does give them a good overall view for spotting any predators that may be creeping up on them (right).

Something in the air

Dogs sniff everything, from the food they eat, to other dogs, especially when it is time to mate. The scent in the air enters the nose and attaches to an organ called the *olfactory bulb*. This is very large and very sensitive in a dog's nose. It then sends signals to the brain.

Olfactory bulb

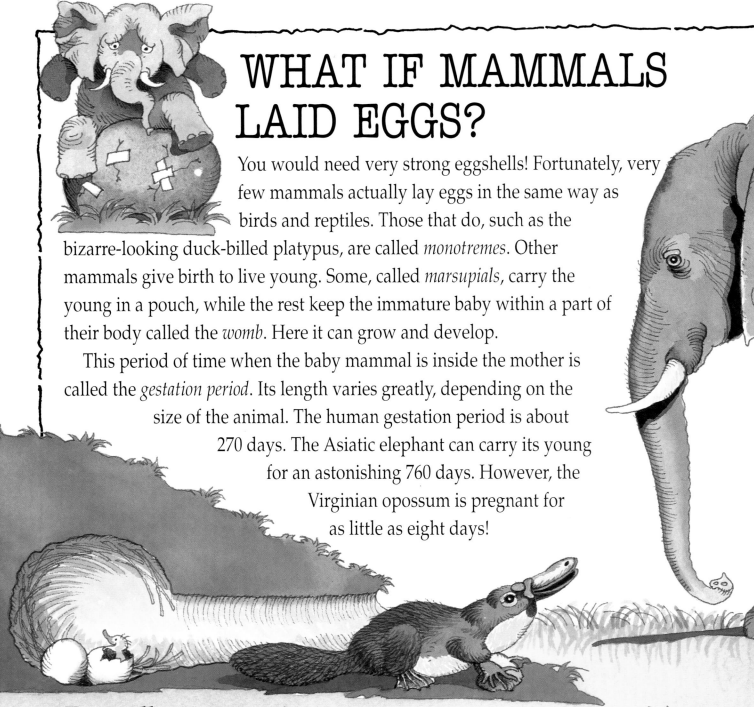

WHAT IF MAMMALS LAID EGGS?

You would need very strong eggshells! Fortunately, very few mammals actually lay eggs in the same way as birds and reptiles. Those that do, such as the bizarre-looking duck-billed platypus, are called *monotremes*. Other mammals give birth to live young. Some, called *marsupials*, carry the young in a pouch, while the rest keep the immature baby within a part of their body called the *womb*. Here it can grow and develop.

This period of time when the baby mammal is inside the mother is called the *gestation period*. Its length varies greatly, depending on the size of the animal. The human gestation period is about 270 days. The Asiatic elephant can carry its young for an astonishing 760 days. However, the Virginian opossum is pregnant for as little as eight days!

Egg-cellent parents!

There are only three species of mammal that actually lay eggs. These are the duck-billed platypus (above), the long-beaked echidna (right), and the short-beaked echidna, which all live in Australasia. The duck-billed platypus usually lays two eggs in an underground den. These eggs are covered in a tough leathery shell to protect them.

After about ten to twelve days in the den, the babies hatch from their eggs and feed on milk. This is produced by special glands on the mother (see page 128).

Womb　　Ovaries

Baby elephant

Birth canal

Eggs without shells

Although most mammals don't lay eggs like birds or reptiles, they all (including humans) produce tiny, microscopic eggs from organs inside the female, called *ovaries*. After mating, these eggs may be fertilized with sperm from the male, they embed themselves into an area of the mother's womb. The baby grows here, protected from the outside world and fed by nutrients that pass from the mother's blood. These nutrients are passed from the mother to the baby through an organ called the *placenta*, and along the umbilical cord. Once the baby has developed enough, it is born. It passes from the womb, through the birth canal, and out into the world.

What if a kangaroo didn't have a pouch on its belly?

It would have to find some other way of carrying around its young. Kangaroos give birth to very immature, furless babies. The tiny creature has to crawl through its mother's fur, into the pouch, where it attaches itself to one of four milk teats.

The pouch is called a *marsupium*, and mammals that have this are referred to as marsupials. These include possums, opossums, koalas, and wombats.

WHAT IF COWS HAD NO UDDERS?

The udders of a cow hold the milk-producing glands, known as *mammary glands*. Mammals are the only animals to have these milk-producing organs to feed their young. The young cow merely has to suck on its mother's teats to be fed with a rich supply of nutrients. These are essential for the calf during the first months of its life. Without udders and teats, the young calves would starve, and we would be without milk to pour over our cereal in the morning!

Milk glands

Udders

What if we drank seal's milk?

We would get very fat indeed! The milk that different mammals produce varies greatly, depending on the needs of the young animal. Seals need to put on a thick layer of fat, called *blubber*, to keep them warm in the cold sea (see page 123). The milk that seal mothers produce is, therefore very high in fat. Cow's and human's has only 4.5%, while seal's milk contains 53.2% fat – not very good if you're on a diet!

Bouncing delivery

When an infant kangaroo (joey) first reaches its mother's pouch after birth, it attaches itself to one of four teats (see page 11). The teat then swells and fixes the joey firmly within the pouch. It remains clamped to the teat for about two months, by which time the mouth has grown enough to release the joey. After another four months, the joey is old enough to leave the pouch, but it still continues to feed on its original teat, even climbing into the pouch when it needs a rest.

Meanwhile, another baby kangaroo may have been born. This, too, will have crawled into its mother's pouch and will be suckling on a different teat. Kangaroos can therefore carry two joeys in their pouch at the same time.

Feeding time
As the joey grows, the milk it drinks from the teat changes. At birth, the milk is very rich in nutrients, which decline as it gets older. With two babies feeding in the pouch, the mother will be producing two different types of milk!

What if baby mammals were left to fend for themselves?

They would become easy food for predators such as wolves, lions, and eagles! Without any parents to take care of them, baby mammals would have to learn to hunt, hide, and forage in order to reach adulthood. Fortunately, mammal parents take more care of their young than any other animals, ensuring that plenty of them get to old age. The parents' first concern is to feed their young. This is done by supplying milk from the mother. They must also teach their babies how to find food, either by hunting or grazing.

As the young grow, the parents must also protect them from any predators that are after an easy snack. This doesn't mean that baby mammals are completely helpless. Some, like antelope, are able to run almost as soon as they are born.

129

WHAT IF A LION HAD NO PRIDE?

It would be very lonely. Lions are the only cats that live in groups, or prides. As with any group of animals, each of the lions has a different role. The females hunt for food and bring up the babies, or cubs. The males defend the females of the pride and the area of land where they live, called the *territory*, from rival males and other prides of lions.

Solitary cats

Apart from the lion, all 34 other kinds of cats – from tigers to wildcats – are mainly solitary. They live and hunt alone. Only during the breeding season when a male and a female are together, and when a mother is with her cubs, do these cats have any company.

Elephants on parade

When moving from place to place, elephants may walk in a long line, like soldiers on parade. The herd is led by the oldest female, or cow, the matriarch. The rest of the herd, including her sisters, daughters, and their babies, rely on her to find food and water.

Rival male

A fully grown male will leave his original pride. He will then wander alone for a while, then try to join another pride, so that he can mate with the females, and father offspring. But first he must challenge the pride's leader.

Leader of the pride

The chief male of the pride defends his females and territory fiercely. He fluffs up his mane to look large and strong, and growls loud and long. He tries to repel the rival by fright first. If this doesn't work, it may come to a real fight!

Female hunters

The older, experienced females are the pride's main hunters. They work together to chase and separate a herd of zebra and wildebeest, then they run down a young, old, or sick member. However, they will let the pride-leading male eat first.

Safety in numbers

Many large plant-eating mammals form herds with others of their kind. Sometimes they form mixed herds too, like zebra with wildebeest and gazelles. These herds can number from a handful to many thousands of animals.

There are many noses and pairs of eyes and ears that can detect any approaching danger. If one herd member spots trouble, it can warn the others. Should a predator approach too closely, the herd panics and runs. The hunter then finds it hard to single out one victim from the blur of bodies, heads, legs, and stripes that flash past very quickly.

Trooping baboons

The baboon is a type of monkey that spends much of its time on the ground. Baboons dwell in groups called *troops*, which can be subdivided into bands, clans, and family groups. The troops can number up to 250 baboons. These are based around the mothers and their children. There are a few males, and the biggest, most senior of these lead the troop from danger or defend it against predators, such as the leopard.

Lion cubs
Females with young cubs guard their offspring and feed them on mother's milk. However, danger may come with a rival male, which will kill any existing cubs if it takes over the pride so that its own can be reared.

Young males
The growing males stay with the pride, as long as they do not threaten the leading male. When they want to have any cubs of their own, then they must either challenge the leading male, or leave and take over another pride.

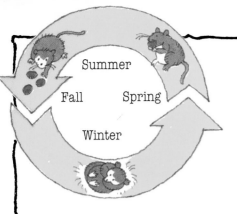

WHAT IF A SQUIRREL DIDN'T STORE ITS NUTS?

The big sleep

Squirrels and many other small mammals sleep for long periods in winter, when the weather is cold and food is scarce. By going to sleep, they are able to slow down the speed at which their body works (see below) and so save energy. To prepare for winter, the mammal has to fatten itself up during fall, before it goes to sleep.

It might starve during the long winter months, when food is hard to find. Many mammals gather food during times of plenty, to hide away and keep, and eat when food is scarce. Squirrels collect fall nuts, such as oak acorns and hazel cobs, and bury them in the ground. Later, the squirrel is only able to find about one-quarter of the nuts it stored, but that's enough to see it through the winter months.

Life in the fast lane

Different mammals live to different ages. In general, bigger mammals live longer. They need the time to grow from a baby to full size. Small mammals, however, live their life faster. Their body processes, such as heartbeat and breathing, are quicker. A shrew's heart beats 800 times a minute, even when it is resting. An elephant's beats a mere 25 times a minute. All this activity and action mean smaller animals "wear out" and die sooner. A shrew aged six months is very old, whereas elephants may live to more than 70 years.

Gliding and Flying

A few small mammals are capable of gliding and even flying. Flying squirrels and gliding possums can swoop, using a flap of skin between their legs, like the wings of a glider.

However, bats are the only mammals that can truly fly. During millions of years of evolution, the bat's arms have developed into wings. The long finger bones hold open a very thin, leathery wing membrane, which the bat flaps to stay in the air.

Membrane

Finger

Going underground

While some small mammals live in the trees, or swoop and soar through the sky, others have chosen to spend their lives underground. A mole tunnels by scraping and pushing aside the soil with its large, powerful, spade-shaped front paws. These have very big, strong claws, like the spikes of a pickax. The mole pushes up extra soil here and there, forming molehills. Tunnels radiate from a central nest, called the *fortress*.

This mammal spends most of its life underground, roaming its existing tunnels and digging new ones, to find food such as earthworms and soil grubs.

Working on the nightshift

Many small mammals, such as bats and rats, are active mainly when it is dark. These nighttime animals are called *nocturnal*. Other mammals, such as monkeys and squirrels are active mostly by day. They are *diurnal*.

Night mammals usually have large eyes to see in the dark, keen noses to smell, extremely sensitive hearing to sense the slightest sound and large whiskers to feel their way. Day mammals, like the bear, only need small eyes to see in the bright sunlight. If these daytime mammals went out in the dark, they would never be able to find their way.

WHAT IF AN ELEPHANT HAD NO TRUNK?

The long trunk is one of the main features of the animal, and it couldn't survive without it. The trunk is the nose and upper lip, that have joined together and grown very long. The elephant uses its trunk for many vital actions, especially eating and drinking. Without a trunk, this plant-eater would not be able to pick up grass and leaves to eat. It also uses the trunk to smell, breathe, feel, and to suck up water. If the elephant crosses a deep river, it can even use its trunk as a snorkel!

Trunk call
The hairy tip of the trunk is very sensitive to touch. The two holes are nostrils that lead to the long nose tube. Through this the elephant breathes and trumpets its calls. Muscles bend the trunk in any direction.

Sniffing and smelling
Elephants lift their trunks high to sniff the air for predators, fire, and other dangers, and to catch the scent of their herd and other creatures. They also smell food before eating it.

The daily grind

Long, thin, sharp, fang-shaped teeth are good for catching, killing, and ripping up meaty prey – but they are no good for chewing or grinding up leaves, grass, fruits, and other plant parts. Herbivores (plant-eaters) need wide, broad, fairly flat teeth to mash and pulp their food thoroughly. This is because plants are made from tough fibers that need to be broken down, so that a herbivore's intestines can extract the nutrients.

Feeding

The elephant has a short neck, so its head cannot reach down to the ground or up to the trees. But the trunk can. It curls around juicy grasses and leaves, rips them off, and stuffs them into its mouth.

Communicating

Elephants touch and stroke their fellow herd members, to greet them and keep up their friendships. They also trumpet and make noises with the help of their trunk. These forms of communication are very important to the herd.

Chewing the cud

Some mammals are able to swallow their food quickly, and then bring it up again to chew over slowly. They are called *ruminants*. They include cows, antelope, and llamas.

When the food is first swallowed it goes into the rumen, the first part of the four-chambered stomach (below). The animal can then bring up this half-digested food, called *cud*, to chew over more leisurely. The cud is then swallowed into the reticulum, and then into the intestines.

Drinking and bathing

The trunk's long nasal tubes allow the elephant to suck up enormous amounts of water. This can then be flung over its back when it wishes to cool off at a watering hole. Alternatively, the elephant may be thirsty, and then it will empty its trunk into its mouth to take a drink.

Small intestine

Rumen

Abomasum

Reticulum

Omasum

WHAT IF A TIGER HAD NO TEETH?

Carnassial teeth

It would soon go hungry and starve. The tiger uses its claws to catch and scratch prey. But it needs its teeth to deliver the deadly bites, and to slice the meat off the bones for eating. The tiger has two main kinds of teeth for these jobs. The long, sharp canines or "fangs" are at the front of the mouth. They stab, wound, and skin the victim, making it bleed, suffocate, and die.

The large, ridge-edged carnassial teeth at the back of the mouth come together like the blades of scissors when the tiger closes its jaws. These very strong teeth carve off and slice up the meat, and can even crunch gristle (cartilage) and soft bones.

Canine teeth

Purr-fect claws

A cat's claws are vital for its survival in the wild. With these incredibly sharp weapons, the hunter can slash, stab, and pin prey that will become its food. However, these deadly claws need to be kept razor sharp for the next kill. To ensure this, most cats can withdraw, or retract, their claws into sheaths in the toes.

This allows the cat to run, walk, and jump without scraping its sharp talons along the ground. It keeps them sharp, unbroken, and clean. It keeps them from getting blunt or getting tangled in twigs, grass, bark, and other things. When the cat needs its claws to climb a tree or to slash and pin its prey, it makes them stick out of the toes.

Claws indoors

The cat's claw is equivalent to your fingernail or toenail. But the claw can swing or pivot on its toe bone. A muscle in the lower leg pulls on a long, stringlike tendon that is attached to the bone and claw. This pulls the sharp claw out of its protective sheath.

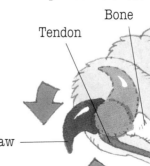

Tendon

Bone

Claw

Plant-eating carnivore

When the giant panda of China was first discovered, it posed a problem to scientists. It has the sharp, fanglike teeth of a carnivore (meat-eater), and is indeed a close relative of the meat-eating raccoon. However, its diet consists almost solely of bamboo shoots. Even though it can eat meat, the panda chooses the young shoots of this type of grass. Unfortunately, bamboo is very low in nutritional value. As a result, it must spend nearly all of its time sitting around, lazily eating in order to consume enough to survive.

Highly-sprung hunter

The fastest hunter on land owes its speed to its flexible backbone. Without this powerful spring running along its spine, the cheetah would not be able to catch and kill the nimble prey that it hunts, such as gazelle and springbok.

As this big cat sprints, the spine flexes, stretching the body out, and allowing the legs to cover even more distance with each stride. This makes the cheetah the world's fastest runner, at over 60 mph (100 km/h).

As the cheetah's legs come together, the spine bends up in the middle.

As the cheetah extends its legs, the spine flattens and arches backward.

As a result the legs can stretch further apart, letting the cheetah run faster.

WHAT IF HUMANS COULD GRIP WITH THEIR FEET?

You could hang upside down from a tree, and do all kinds of other exciting activities. But you might not be able to run and jump so easily. Human feet are designed for walking, and human hands for holding. Our monkey and ape cousins spend most of their time in trees, so they don't need to walk. Instead, all their limbs can grip like hands. Some monkeys are even able to grip with their tails!

Orangutan
These great orange apes live in the densest, steamiest rainforests of Southeast Asia. They rarely come to the ground, and they can bend their legs at almost any angle from the body.

What if apes could stand upright?

One close cousin of the great apes spends most of its time upright. That's us! The true great apes, however, are not able to stand for long. The gorilla spends much of the day on the ground. It usually walks on all fours, on its feet and hand-knuckles. Males sometimes stand upright and charge, if they are threatened by an intruder. Chimps and orangutans can walk upright in order to carry things like fruit, sticks, or rocks. But they can only keep this up for short distances.

Gibbon
The gibbons of Southeast Asia are the champion tree-swingers. They hang from branches by their hooklike hands and powerful arms, and move by swinging from tree to tree with astonishing speed. Because of this, their arms are much longer and stronger than their legs.

What if there were no sea mammals?

Mammals are some of the largest creatures swimming throughout the waters of the world. Whales, dolphins, seals, and otters eat a massive amount of fish, krill, and other sea animals. Without mammals, there would certainly be a lot more fish around (especially because humans eat a vast quantity of fish every day!).

Other predators, such as sharks, would need to find alternative sources of food. However, there are plenty of other fish to eat. In fact, mammals only make up a small percentage of sea creatures, so if they had never existed, they wouldn't be missed all that much.

Insects

Some insects, such as mosquitoes, feed on the blood of mammals. Without mammals, they would have to find something else that they could eat.

Birds

Several species have been hunted to extinction by mammals, such as the diatryma and the elephant bird. If mammals had never been around, these birds could still be alive.

Molluscs

These creatures are incredibly successful and numerous in the sea, from sea snails to cuttlefish and squid. They provide food for both whales and dolphins. If they weren't eaten, they would be even more successful.

On top of the world

Without mammals there wouldn't be any humans. Scientists have pondered whether any other group of animal could produce a species as intelligent as ourselves. The favorites to fill the empty space might be the reptiles. They have already dominated the Earth once, during the reign of the dinosaurs. Some believe if they did not die out, then the world could be populated by highly intelligent, bipedal (two legged) lizards.

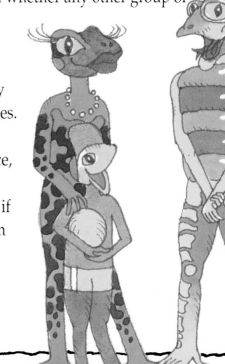

143

THE CRAZY WORLD OF ?WHAT IF...

SHARKS

CONTENTS

WHAT IF SHARKS WERE THE ONLY FISH?

Sharks form the pinnacle of an enormous food chain that exists in the world's oceans. This includes a whole host of creatures, from the smallest plankton and coral polyps to the largest fish and mammals. These incredibly diverse animals are dependent upon each other for survival. If sharks were the only fish, then there would be nothing for them to eat. They would very quickly starve and die out.

Food chain

Life in the oceans provides an endless cycle of nutrients, beginning with the tiniest, microscopic creatures. These are eaten by larger plankton, shrimp, and small fish, which in turn are eaten by larger fish, such as fry and herring. Finally, we reach the great predators, such as sharks.

When sharks die, their bodies provide food for the microscopic life. So the cycle of nutrients begins again.

What if sharks didn't have teeth?

Most sharks usually have a bristling array of very sharp teeth, set in a jaw that can be chomped together by extremely powerful muscles. These teeth are continuously replaced when they have fallen out. As the old ones fall out, new, sharper teeth that were growing behind take their place.

However, the biggest sharks, the whale shark and the basking shark, have almost no teeth at all. Instead their teeth are extremely small, and in order to eat they have to strain shrimp or plankton from the water.

Tuna

Plankton

Small fry and shrimp

Herring

Aquatic zoo

Many fish have been named after other animals because they share certain characteristics. For example, the catfish has long whiskers which it uses to feel around for food. Sea horses are unlike any other fish. They swim in an upright position with their heads bowed – like a prancing horse. The lionfish has a large mane of spines, which are tipped with a powerful poison. However, the dogfish doesn't look much like its land-living canine counterpart!

When is a fish not a fish?

Just as many fish have been named after other animals, so many animals have been called fish! For example, starfish belong to a group of animals called *echinoderms*, which includes sea cucumbers. Crayfish are, in fact, crustaceans, relatives of lobsters and crabs. Cuttlefish are mollusks and are similar to octopus and squid.

Some sea animals have evolved to look very similar to fish, such as whales and dolphins. These have developed the same sleek body shape as fish, but they are mammals.

Crayfish

Starfish

Cuttlefish

WHAT IF A HERRING DIDN'T HAVE SCALES?

A fish without scales would have much less protection against the teeth and spines of predators and enemies. It would be attacked by pests, such as fish lice and other blood-sucking parasites. It could be rubbed and cut by stones or sharp-leafed water plants. The scales of a fish act as a protective coat of armor against the outside world. Most scales are arranged like the shingles of a roof. One edge of the scale, the stalk, is attached to the skin, while the rest of the scale lies flat against the one beneath.

Some fish, like eels, have scales that are hidden by a thick, tough, slimy skin which lies on top of the scales.

Smooth customer
Fish scales are usually arranged with the stalk pointing toward the front. This lets the fish slip through the water.

Flow of water

Tough as old boots

Sharks are covered in special scales called denticles. These are tiny hooks, or teeth, that are embedded in the skin and point backward, making shark's skin extremely abrasive (rough).

They also make the skin extremely hard-wearing. So much so that jackets, vests, belts and even shoes can be made from this tough and highly durable skin.

What if a fish had no skeleton?

Fish can be split into two different groups. Those that have a skeleton made from bone, known as bony fish, and those whose skeleton is made from gristle, or cartilage, known as cartilaginous fish. Even though skeletons vary (right), they are all based on the long spinal column in the middle of the body. This is made of linked parts called vertebrae. From this ribs grow, and at the front is the skull.

The skeleton forms the fish's inner framework, upon which all of its internal organs, skin, and muscles sit. Without it, a fish would be a blob of soft tissue.

Skull

Ribs

Fin rays

Spinal column

No-bone fish
Not all fish have a skeleton made out of bone. Sharks, skates, rays, and chimaeras (e.g. ratfishes) have a skeleton made of cartilage or gristle (left). It's very strong and tough, like bone, but more flexible. These fish are called *cartilaginous fish* or chondrichthyes, and there are about 800 kinds or species.

How can you tell the age of a fish?

Most fish keep growing through life, so the biggest fish of a species are the oldest. Some types of fish, such as salmon, have scales with tiny dark lines on them. These are growth rings. Like the growth rings in a tree trunk, they tell you not only the age of a fish, but also how it has grown through its life. A group of dark lines close together shows the slow growth of one winter. A group of lines that are farther apart indicates faster growth during the summer months.

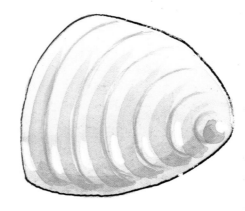

WHAT IF FISH COULD FLY?

Most fish move by swimming through the water, either by wiggling their body from side to side, or by waving their fins. A few have learned how to use their fins to walk on land (see page 153). Other fish have developed the ability to leap from the water and swoop and glide above the surface for several feet, before plunging back down into the waves. They are called flying fish.

Take off
If they are threatened by a predator, such as a shark, flying fish will gather speed, up to 20 mph (32 km/h), and shoot above the waves.

What if you could ride a sea horse?

Sea horses are true fish, cousins of pipefish and sticklebacks, but with a very strange body shape. The face resembles a horse's head, with small pectoral fins sticking from the neck, one dorsal fin on the back of the stiff body, and a curly tail to wrap around plants or rocks to hold the fish in place. Instead of getting forward movement by swishing its tail, the sea horse waves its dorsal fin very quickly to move itself forward. By swimming at a modest speed, the sea horse can suck or snap any food into its small, tube-shaped mouth.

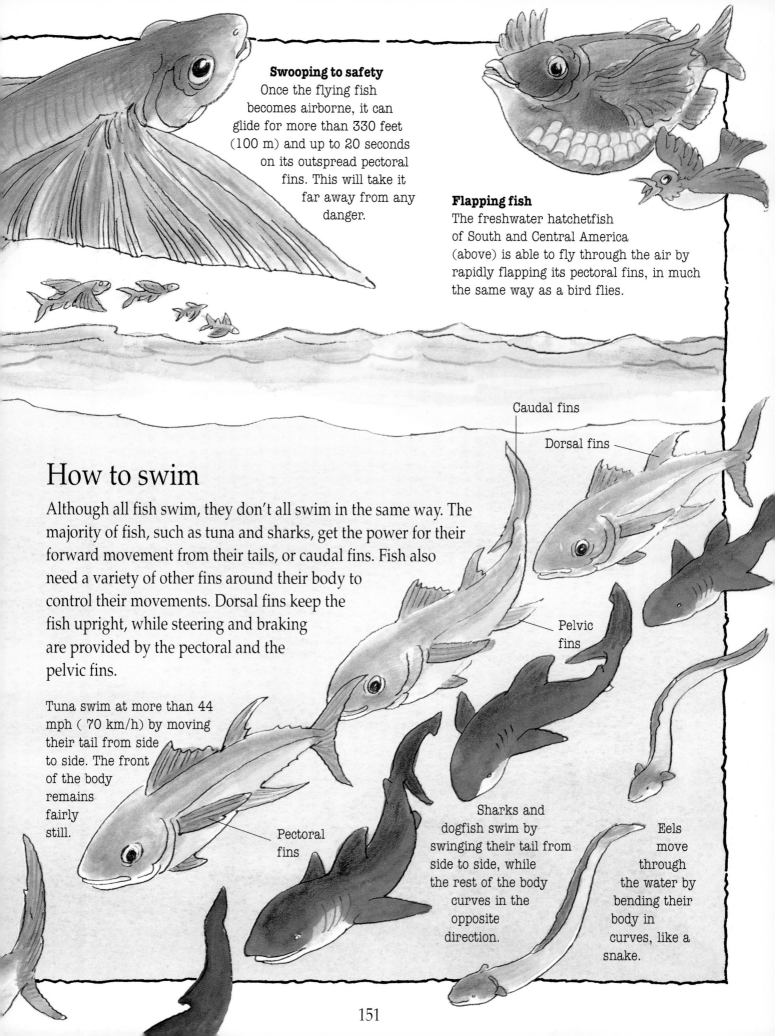

Swooping to safety
Once the flying fish becomes airborne, it can glide for more than 330 feet (100 m) and up to 20 seconds on its outspread pectoral fins. This will take it far away from any danger.

Flapping fish
The freshwater hatchetfish of South and Central America (above) is able to fly through the air by rapidly flapping its pectoral fins, in much the same way as a bird flies.

How to swim

Although all fish swim, they don't all swim in the same way. The majority of fish, such as tuna and sharks, get the power for their forward movement from their tails, or caudal fins. Fish also need a variety of other fins around their body to control their movements. Dorsal fins keep the fish upright, while steering and braking are provided by the pectoral and the pelvic fins.

Caudal fins

Dorsal fins

Pelvic fins

Tuna swim at more than 44 mph (70 km/h) by moving their tail from side to side. The front of the body remains fairly still.

Pectoral fins

Sharks and dogfish swim by swinging their tail from side to side, while the rest of the body curves in the opposite direction.

Eels move through the water by bending their body in curves, like a snake.

151

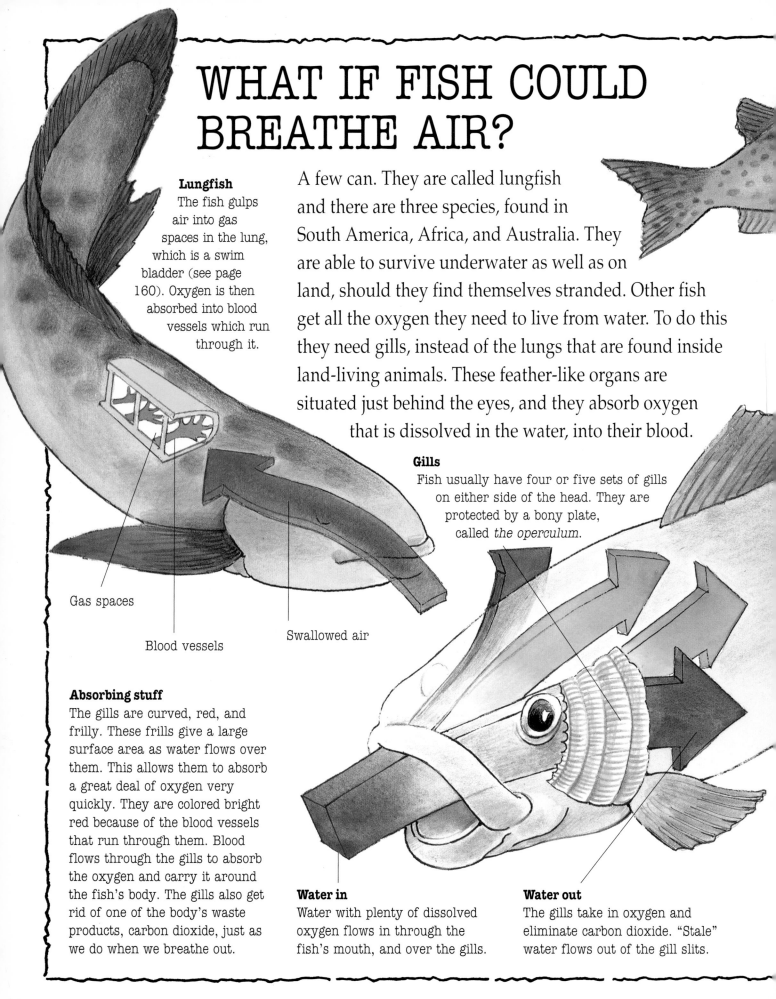

WHAT IF FISH COULD BREATHE AIR?

A few can. They are called lungfish and there are three species, found in South America, Africa, and Australia. They are able to survive underwater as well as on land, should they find themselves stranded. Other fish get all the oxygen they need to live from water. To do this they need gills, instead of the lungs that are found inside land-living animals. These feather-like organs are situated just behind the eyes, and they absorb oxygen that is dissolved in the water, into their blood.

Lungfish
The fish gulps air into gas spaces in the lung, which is a swim bladder (see page 160). Oxygen is then absorbed into blood vessels which run through it.

Gas spaces

Blood vessels

Swallowed air

Gills
Fish usually have four or five sets of gills on either side of the head. They are protected by a bony plate, called *the operculum*.

Absorbing stuff
The gills are curved, red, and frilly. These frills give a large surface area as water flows over them. This allows them to absorb a great deal of oxygen very quickly. They are colored bright red because of the blood vessels that run through them. Blood flows through the gills to absorb the oxygen and carry it around the fish's body. The gills also get rid of one of the body's waste products, carbon dioxide, just as we do when we breathe out.

Water in
Water with plenty of dissolved oxygen flows in through the fish's mouth, and over the gills.

Water out
The gills take in oxygen and eliminate carbon dioxide. "Stale" water flows out of the gill slits.

A fish out of water

Several kinds of fish can survive out of water for a short time, and even move across land. They are usually fish that live in tropical swamps, such as catfish, where the pools disappear in the dry season.

The water in these pools is warm and stagnant, with little dissolved oxygen. So the catfish gulps air into pockets in the sides of the gill chambers. Oxygen goes from the air bubbles, through the watery covering of the gills, and into the blood. The gills must always be kept moist. If they dry out, the fish suffocates and dies.

Catfish
These whiskered fish, such as the upside down catfish, will travel over land, in order to get from one pond to another.

Eels
The eel wriggles through grass and plants, taking in extra oxygen through its moist, slimy, almost scaleless skin.

Mudskippers
The mudskipper lives along muddy tropical shores. It has very large gill chambers and refreshes the water in these every few minutes. It can walk on its armlike pectoral fins or surf across mud with its tail.

Bubble and squeak

Although they can't scream and shout, many fish can make noises. They do this by squeezing air bubbles that they have swallowed through their swim bladder, in just the same way as your stomach rumbles from time to time. They can also make noises by rubbing together bones or fin spines.

The sounds may be to frighten enemies, attract mates, or keep in touch with neighbors. Some of these noisy fish are named after the sound they produce, such as drumfish, squeaker catfish, grunter gurnards, snorter horsemackerels, and singing midshipmen.

153

WHAT IF A LANTERN-FISH COULDN'T SEE?

Sight is only one of the impressive array of senses that fish use to detect the underwater world, and is only really useful in the bright, sunlit surface waters. Fish from the dim and murky midwater, between 660 and 3,300 feet (200 and 1,000 m) deep, such as the lantern fish, may have even larger eyes, to let in as much light as possible. To survive in these darker waters, as well as in the completely black depths, fish must employ their other senses to detect the world around them. Some deepsea and cavefish are totally blind and so rely entirely on their other senses. These senses include smell to scent blood in the water, touch to detect changes in currents or approaching fish, and even detection by using electrical currents.

Lens

Cornea

Retina

Lateral line

Fish eyes
Light enters the fish's eye through the transparent domed cornea. It is then bent or focused by a very thick lens, and shines onto the retina. This turns the picture into nerve signals and sends these along a nerve to the brain.

How do fish feel?

Fish can feel in the same way as humans, by detecting any direct touches on their body and fins.

They can also feel currents, swirls, and vibrations coming through the water. These are detected by the silvery stripe that runs along each side of the fish's body, called the *lateral line*. These are incredibly sensitive, and tell the fish about any underwater sounds and movements, and about the position of nearby objects. The fish can use them to sense predators or prey, and avoid bumping into rocks, even in the total darkness of the deep sea.

A shocking experience

Some fish use shocks of electricity to find their way, repel enemies, or stun victims (see page 15). These include the elephant-snout fish, the knifefish and torpedo-rays.

The elephant-snout fish uses electricity as a means of sensing. It makes a weak electrical field around itself by sending out pulses of electricity from its special organs. Its nose and tail detect the field, which is bent or altered by the presence of nearby creatures, rocks, and other objects. They can also detect the tiny electric charges made by another animal's muscles as it moves nearby. The elephant-snout fish grubs in the mud on the bottom and finds food such as water snails and worms, even in cloudy water.

Smelling something fishy!

Sharks use scent to detect their prey. They can "smell" certain substances in the water, even in very tiny quantities. A shark can detect the smallest drop of blood and, thinking it may be a wounded animal, may swim over looking for a meal!

Other fish use their noses to sniff out their food, as well as to recognize other fish of the same species. They are also able to tell the difference between water plants, and even the waters from different streams.

WHAT IF AN ANGLER WENT FISHING?

Fish have developed an array of different adaptations. These range from poisonous spines to inflatable bodies! They can be used either to catch something to eat, or to stop the fish from being eaten.

Anglerfish are a family of fish with a long, fleshy pole (barbel) growing from their forehead. The barbel can be colored, or even illuminated. The anglerfish goes fishing with this barbel to lure unwary prey.

Living seaweed

The leafy sea horse looks as much like a piece of seaweed as a fish. Its body is covered in leaf-like growths. When this sea horse lies still in seaweed, it is virtually impossible to spot, allowing it to hide from any predators.

Swimming plants

Many fish are masters of camouflage, hiding themselves from their prey or predators. Some have developed to look like plants. For example, pipefish (see page 159) are very thin and hang among the leaves of eelgrass, making themselves almost invisible. Those fish that cannot hide themselves have to use speed and agility to escape from being somebody's lunch.

Wobbegong

The frill around the jaw of this shark ensures that it remains hidden from its prey until the last moment. It lurks on the seabed, waiting for a scrap of food to come along.

Don't touch!

Electric eel

Not content with camouflage or fast swimming to avoid predators or catch prey, some fish have developed more aggressive ways to hunt or protect themselves. The electric eel and the electric catfish are able to produce intense bursts of electricity from special organs in their body, in order to stun their prey.

Others, such as the stonefish and the lionfish, have a number of poisonous spines to deter any would-be predators.

Stonefish

What if fish could blow themselves up?

There are some fish which can blow themselves up. When it is swimming about normally, the porcupinefish is covered in sharp spines to deter any would-be attackers. For extra protection, however, the fish is able to fill itself with water, inflating to become a prickly ball – not much of a tasty morsel!

Fishy cleaning staff

Cleaner wrasses are small, black-and-white striped fish which have an unusual occupation in the fish world. By performing a certain dance, the wrasse attracts other fish over to it, then proceeds to "clean" them, removing parasites from their skin and gills. The wrasse even swims into the fish's mouth without coming to harm.

Another fish, the blenny, looks very similar to the wrasse, and even attracts fish using the same dance. However, when the fish approaches, the blenny quickly darts forward and bites a chunk out of its unsuspecting visitor.

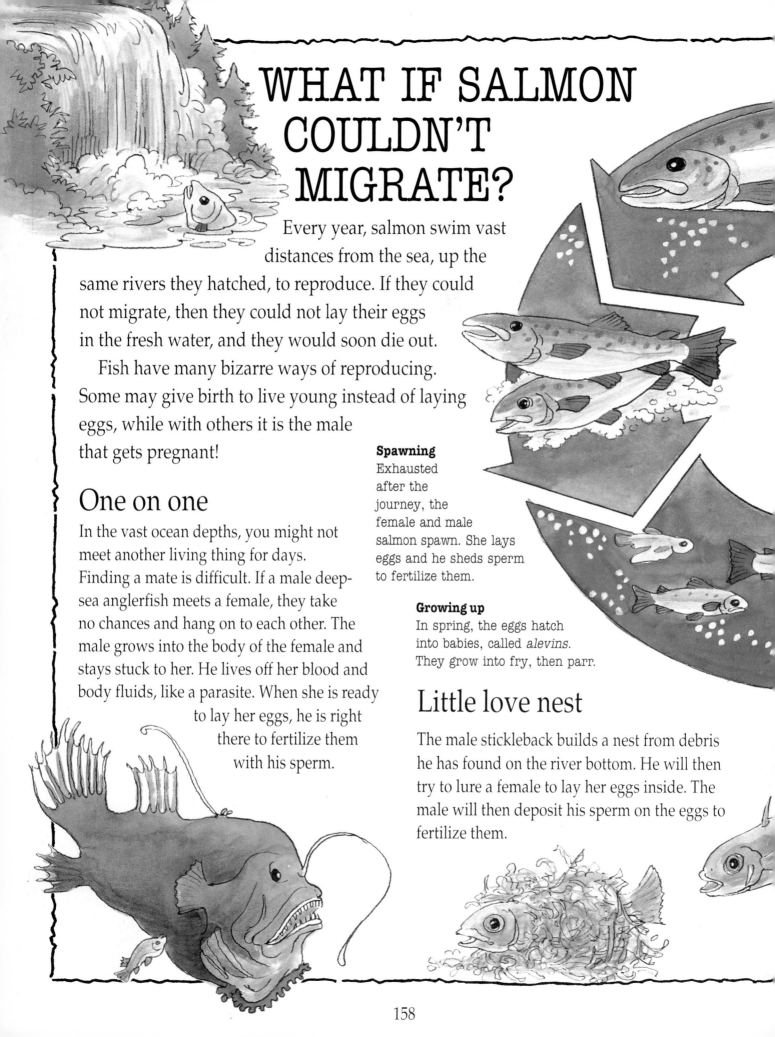

WHAT IF SALMON COULDN'T MIGRATE?

Every year, salmon swim vast distances from the sea, up the same rivers they hatched, to reproduce. If they could not migrate, then they could not lay their eggs in the fresh water, and they would soon die out.

Fish have many bizarre ways of reproducing. Some may give birth to live young instead of laying eggs, while with others it is the male that gets pregnant!

One on one

In the vast ocean depths, you might not meet another living thing for days. Finding a mate is difficult. If a male deep-sea anglerfish meets a female, they take no chances and hang on to each other. The male grows into the body of the female and stays stuck to her. He lives off her blood and body fluids, like a parasite. When she is ready to lay her eggs, he is right there to fertilize them with his sperm.

Spawning
Exhausted after the journey, the female and male salmon spawn. She lays eggs and he sheds sperm to fertilize them.

Growing up
In spring, the eggs hatch into babies, called *alevins*. They grow into fry, then parr.

Little love nest

The male stickleback builds a nest from debris he has found on the river bottom. He will then try to lure a female to lay her eggs inside. The male will then deposit his sperm on the eggs to fertilize them.

The long swim home

The full-grown salmon swims back against the current of the stream in which it was born. It will probably have to negotiate many obstacles, including canal locks and waterfalls.

Staying at sea

Salmon may live at sea for up to five years. During this time, they grow large and sleek.

Leaving home

After four years, the parr turn silvery and become smolts. They head downriver, and out to sea.

What if males had babies?

The males of some fish, such as sea horses and pipefish, gather eggs, which have been laid by the female and look after them while they develop. The male keeps the eggs protected in a pocketlike part on his body made of flaps of skin, called the *brood pouch*. When the babies hatch, they swim out of the pouch opening.

Open wide

Some cichlid fish have a peculiar way of looking after their offspring. They care for both the eggs and babies in their mouth. They are known as mouth-brooders.

When the baby cichlids have hatched, they swim in a cloud around their parent. When danger appears, the cloud of babies swims straight back into the safety of the parent's mouth.

A live birth

Most fish lay eggs, from which their young hatch. This includes sharks, whose eggs are large and in leathery cases with trailing tendrils. Empty egg cases of sharks, skates, and rays are sometimes washed up on the beach as "mermaids' purses." Other sharks, such as the white-tip shark, have eggs that hatch inside the mother, and the young emerge from the reproductive opening, called the *cloaca*.

WHAT IF SHARKS STOPPED SWIMMING?

They would sink to the bottom and stay there. Most fish have an inner body part like an adjustable gas bag, called a swim bladder. The fish adjusts the amount of gas in the bladder to float up or down. Sharks and other cartilaginous fish lack swim bladders and can only stay up by swimming, using their rigid fins like a plane's wings.

Some sharks need to keep swimming to get oxygen from the water into their blood. There are, however, some sharks, like some fish, that can move water over their gills without swimming thereby getting the oxygen into their blood.

Stomach

Gills

Brain

Mouth

Heart

Liver

Which fish have wings but cannot fly?

Rays and skates are flattened cartilaginous fish. Their bodies have developed into a squashed, wing-shaped form. This is perfect for their bottom-dwelling lifestyle, where they scavenge or eat seabed creatures. While skates have a tail they can use to swim like other fish, a ray cannot swish its body from side to side, so it flaps its wings up and down to "fly" through the water.

The largest ray is the Pacific manta or devilfish. It has a "wingspan" of more than 20 feet (6 m) – about the same as a hang-glider – and weighs almost two tons. Stingrays have a sharp spine sticking out of the tail, which they can jab into enemies to inject terrible stinging poison.

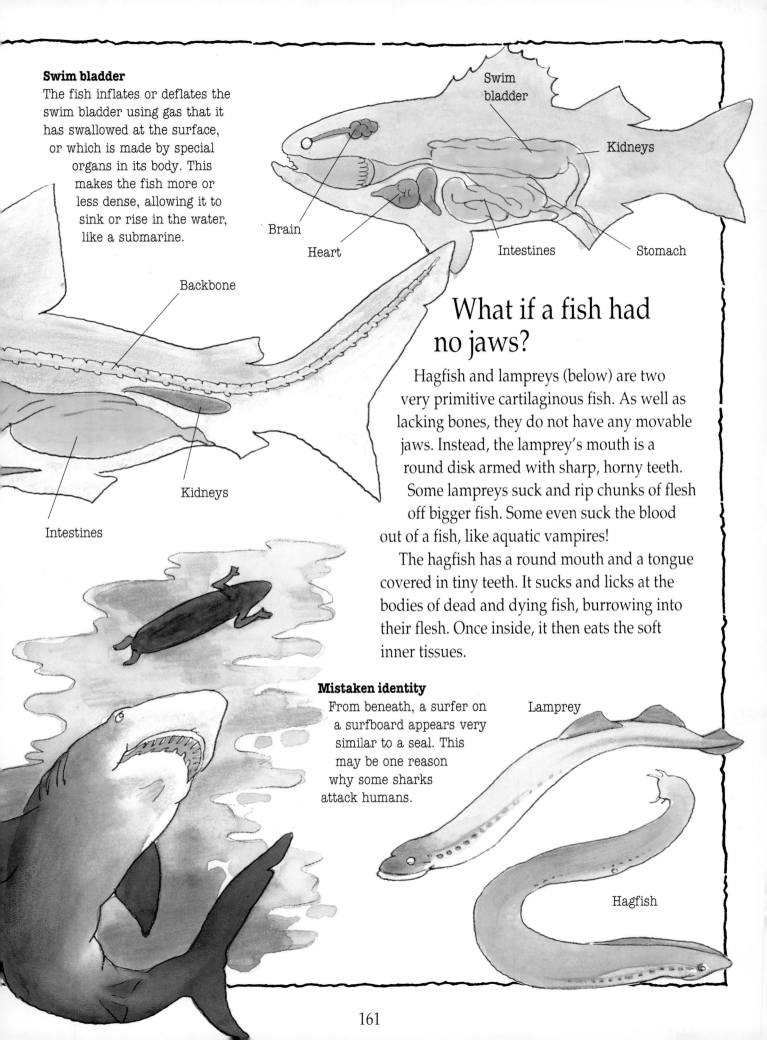

Swim bladder

The fish inflates or deflates the swim bladder using gas that it has swallowed at the surface, or which is made by special organs in its body. This makes the fish more or less dense, allowing it to sink or rise in the water, like a submarine.

Swim bladder

Kidneys

Brain

Heart

Intestines

Stomach

Backbone

Kidneys

Intestines

What if a fish had no jaws?

Hagfish and lampreys (below) are two very primitive cartilaginous fish. As well as lacking bones, they do not have any movable jaws. Instead, the lamprey's mouth is a round disk armed with sharp, horny teeth. Some lampreys suck and rip chunks of flesh off bigger fish. Some even suck the blood out of a fish, like aquatic vampires!

The hagfish has a round mouth and a tongue covered in tiny teeth. It sucks and licks at the bodies of dead and dying fish, burrowing into their flesh. Once inside, it then eats the soft inner tissues.

Mistaken identity

From beneath, a surfer on a surfboard appears very similar to a seal. This may be one reason why some sharks attack humans.

Lamprey

Hagfish

WHAT IF A SEAFISH SWAM IN FRESH WATER?

Altogether, there are about 8,500 species of freshwater fish that swim in the many streams, rivers, and lakes throughout the world. These include the trout, the perch, and the fearsome pike.

Freshwater fish and seafish have developed bodies to cope with their own environments. There are very few fish that can live in both. If a seafish tried to swim in fresh water, it would blow up like a balloon.

Shriveled fish
A freshwater fish placed in saltwater would shrivel up. Even though it would be surrounded by water, a freshwater fish would find the sea too salty and could not control the water balance of its own body. It would rapidly lose its body fluids and die.

Giants of the rivers

The size of some freshwater fish is only governed by the availability of food and the space they are given to live in. With a lot to eat and roam in, some fish have grown to giant proportions. The arapaima of the Amazon river can reach a length of nearly 10 feet (3 m), and there are stories of it eating small children! Other river giants include the pla beuk which swims in the water of the Mekong river in China. It can grow over 10 feet (3 m), and weighs more than 530 lbs (240 kg) – that's over three times the weight of an adult human! At the other end of the scale is the Chagos dwarf goby, which is only 0.3 inches (8 mm) long.

What if fish could live in seas and rivers?

A few fish found in fresh water are able to survive in the salty sea. Salmon feed and grow in the ocean before swimming up the same river in which they were born, in order to spawn.

Common eels are actually born in the middle of the ocean. They then spend a couple of years drifting on the ocean currents, before swimming up rivers to feed and grow into adults, and then return to the sea.

Sturgeon

Salmon

Eel

Brown trout

Stealth-hunter

Pike are vicious hunters found in most northern lakes and rivers. Their slender bodies make them particularly speedy through tranquil waters. The larger pikes feed on fish, birds, and even mammals!

Hunters of rivers and lakes

As with sharks in the sea, freshwater habitats have their own hunters. In fact, there are cases in which sharks have swam into river estuaries to feed on the fish there!

Bull sharks are renowned for this, and have even attacked people who thought they were safe in the freshwater estuaries of rivers.

Other fishy hunters, like piranha, swarm together in large, powerful schools, looking for something to eat. If they come across a fish or other animal that shows signs of being wounded or in trouble, these fish will attack, and eat the creatures in a matter of seconds.

WHAT IF CORAL DIDN'T BUILD REEFS?

We wouldn't have some of the richest and most colorful wildlife habitats on the planet, and the many fish that populate the reefs would be left without a home. Reefs are massive natural structures that are built by tiny animals, called coral polyps. The Great Barrier Reef, off the coast of Australia, stretches over 2,000 km (1,250 miles).

The reef forms only one of many coastal environments, which can also include mudflats, sandbanks, rocky shores, and beaches. The shallow waters are packed full of food, such as seaweeds and invertebrate (backbone-less) animals that a huge diversity of fish, from clownfish to sharks, can feed on.

Biodiversity
A patch of seashore in North America or Europe might have 50 different fish species. A same-sized patch of tropical coral reef could have 500, as well as other animals, from anemones to starfish.

What if a fish had a beak?

The parrotfish found swimming around many coral reefs is so called because it has a hard, horny mouth, rather like the beak of a parrot. This has been formed by the fish's teeth that have fused together.

The parrotfish uses its hard mouth to scrape at the stony skeletons that the coral have left behind. It does not feed on the rock itself, but on the tiny coral animals and other small creatures. As the fish clears a patch and moves on, new coral polyps and other creatures settle on the exposed rock. The whole process usually balances out, so while the fish is feeding itself, the coral polyps continue to build the reef.

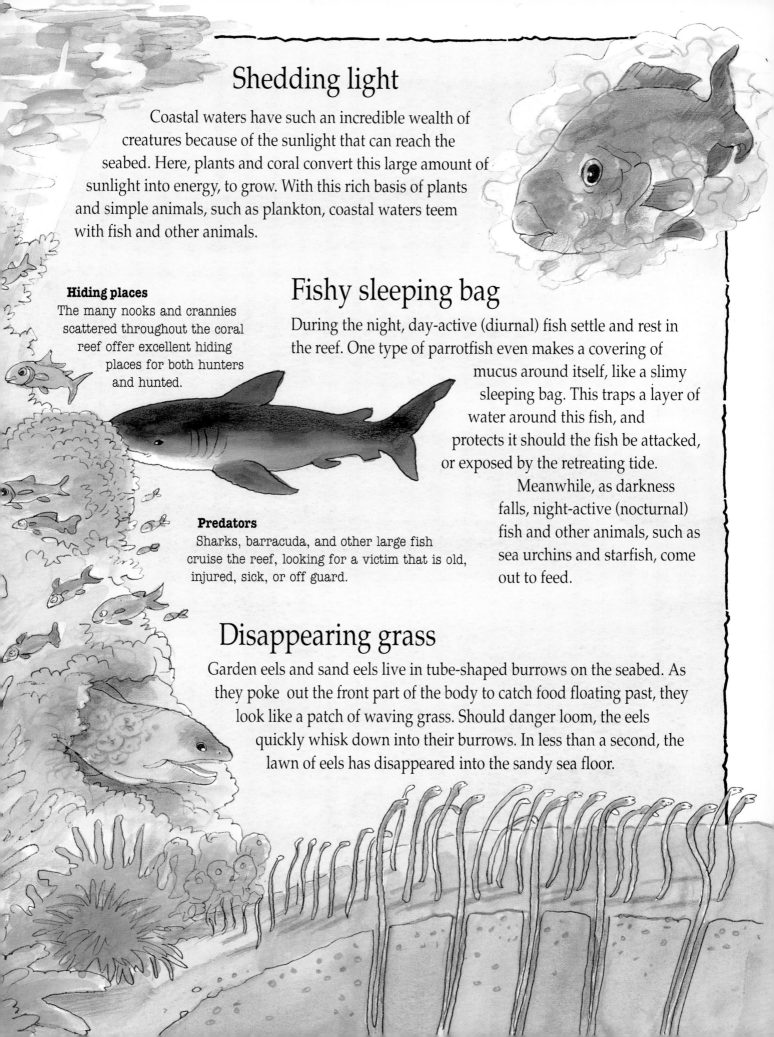

Shedding light

Coastal waters have such an incredible wealth of creatures because of the sunlight that can reach the seabed. Here, plants and coral convert this large amount of sunlight into energy, to grow. With this rich basis of plants and simple animals, such as plankton, coastal waters teem with fish and other animals.

Hiding places

The many nooks and crannies scattered throughout the coral reef offer excellent hiding places for both hunters and hunted.

Fishy sleeping bag

During the night, day-active (diurnal) fish settle and rest in the reef. One type of parrotfish even makes a covering of mucus around itself, like a slimy sleeping bag. This traps a layer of water around this fish, and protects it should the fish be attacked, or exposed by the retreating tide.

Meanwhile, as darkness falls, night-active (nocturnal) fish and other animals, such as sea urchins and starfish, come out to feed.

Predators

Sharks, barracuda, and other large fish cruise the reef, looking for a victim that is old, injured, sick, or off guard.

Disappearing grass

Garden eels and sand eels live in tube-shaped burrows on the seabed. As they poke out the front part of the body to catch food floating past, they look like a patch of waving grass. Should danger loom, the eels quickly whisk down into their burrows. In less than a second, the lawn of eels has disappeared into the sandy sea floor.

WHAT IF FISH DIDN'T SWIM IN SCHOOLS?

They might easily be caught and eaten by one of the ocean's many hunters! Some species of fish, particularly those found in the open ocean, such as cod and herring, form themselves into enormous groups called *shoals*, or schools. These schools can have as few as 25 individuals, or as many as several thousand fish, all of them swimming in the same direction. These schools have nothing to do with education. Instead, the dense collections of fish protect themselves by dazzling the hunter with a silvery blur. Other open-water fish have developed weapons or incredible speed to avoid predators or catch their prey.

Open ocean sword-fighter

The swordfish has a long, sharp, pointed nose, much like a sword. It uses this to defend itself, and also to stun and kill its prey with slashing strokes. The sharp nose also helps to make the fish extremely streamlined, allowing it to slice through the water at very high speeds.

Underwater pilots

The pilotfish swims very near other large sea animals, such as sharks, giving the impression that it is guiding the bigger creature. This is not the case. Instead, this small, striped fish merely follows the creature around the water. It can feed on any scraps of food that the shark leaves after it has made a kill. Pilotfish are extremely agile and so can easily dodge a lumbering shark if it tries to eat them.

What is the fastest fish?

The fastest fish in the world live in the oceans, far from shore. They need their speed either to dodge predators or catch prey. Over short distances the sailfish is the quickest thing in the water. In short bursts, it can swim at an amazing speed of nearly 70 mph (110 km/h). To achieve this, its body needs to be extremely streamlined, otherwise the turbulence it creates in the water would slow it down. The streamlining is further enhanced by its almost scaleless skin. In parts of the body where there are scales, they are set well below the skin's surface to prevent them causing turbulence. Other very fast fish include the wahoo and the blue-fin tuna. These can swim at more than 40 mph (65 km/h).

Sailfish

Wahoo

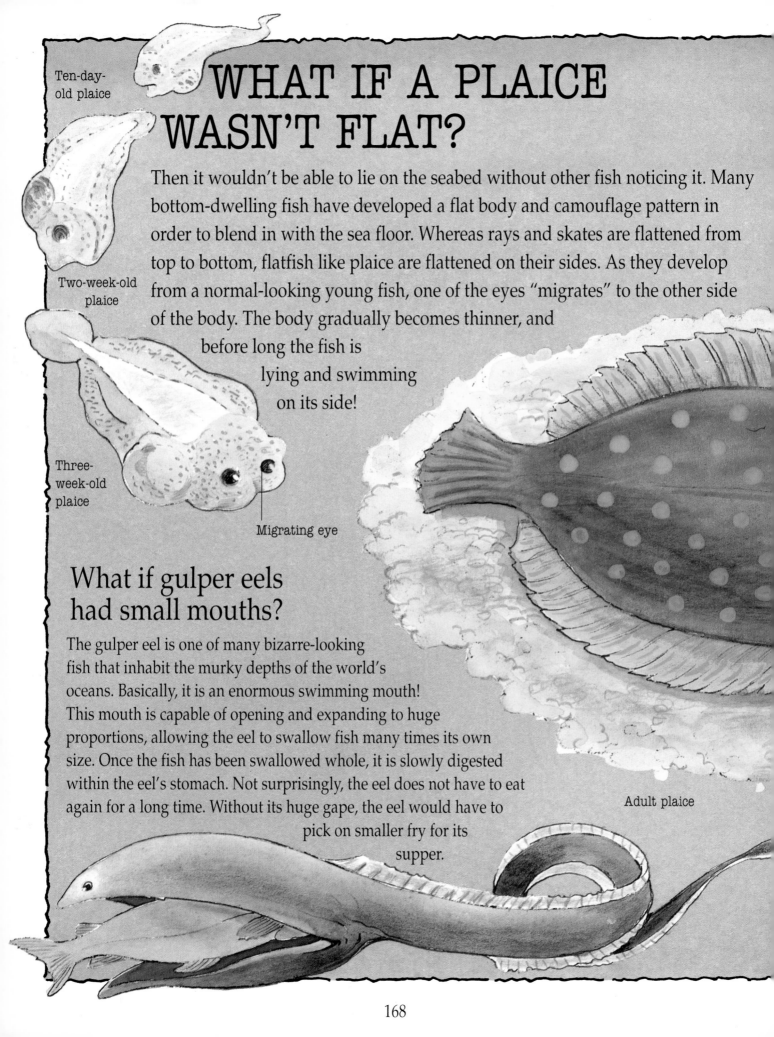

Ten-day-old plaice

Two-week-old plaice

Three-week-old plaice

Migrating eye

WHAT IF A PLAICE WASN'T FLAT?

Then it wouldn't be able to lie on the seabed without other fish noticing it. Many bottom-dwelling fish have developed a flat body and camouflage pattern in order to blend in with the sea floor. Whereas rays and skates are flattened from top to bottom, flatfish like plaice are flattened on their sides. As they develop from a normal-looking young fish, one of the eyes "migrates" to the other side of the body. The body gradually becomes thinner, and before long the fish is lying and swimming on its side!

What if gulper eels had small mouths?

The gulper eel is one of many bizarre-looking fish that inhabit the murky depths of the world's oceans. Basically, it is an enormous swimming mouth! This mouth is capable of opening and expanding to huge proportions, allowing the eel to swallow fish many times its own size. Once the fish has been swallowed whole, it is slowly digested within the eel's stomach. Not surprisingly, the eel does not have to eat again for a long time. Without its huge gape, the eel would have to pick on smaller fry for its supper.

Adult plaice

Fish on stilts

The tripod fish gets its name from the three highly developed fins that hang beneath its body. When the tripod fish isn't swimming through the dark deep ocean, it rests on the seabed. It uses its elongated fins like a set of stilts, keeping its body above the slimy ooze and mud that coat the sea floor.

Once on the seabed, the tripod fish can "walk" along the bottom, as it waits for any morsels of food to come along. Other fish that rest and "walk" on their fins are lizardfish and some types of gurnards.

Now you see me, now you don't!
Some bottom-dwelling flatfish, such as plaice, can vary the color of their skin, just like a chameleon! They can blend in with the sea floor, and lie undisturbed by predators.

What if fish had flashlights?

Nearly 80% of all fish found in the darkness of the deep sea are able to produce light from special organs on their bodies.

Some, such as deep-sea anglerfish and viperfish, use a light on the end of a pole to lure prey (see page 156). Others, such as lantern fish and hatchetfish, use downward pointing light organs in order to blend in with any sunlight that filters down from above. This will keep them camouflaged from predators that may be swimming below. Some fish use their lights in order to frighten off other fish that may eat them for lunch.

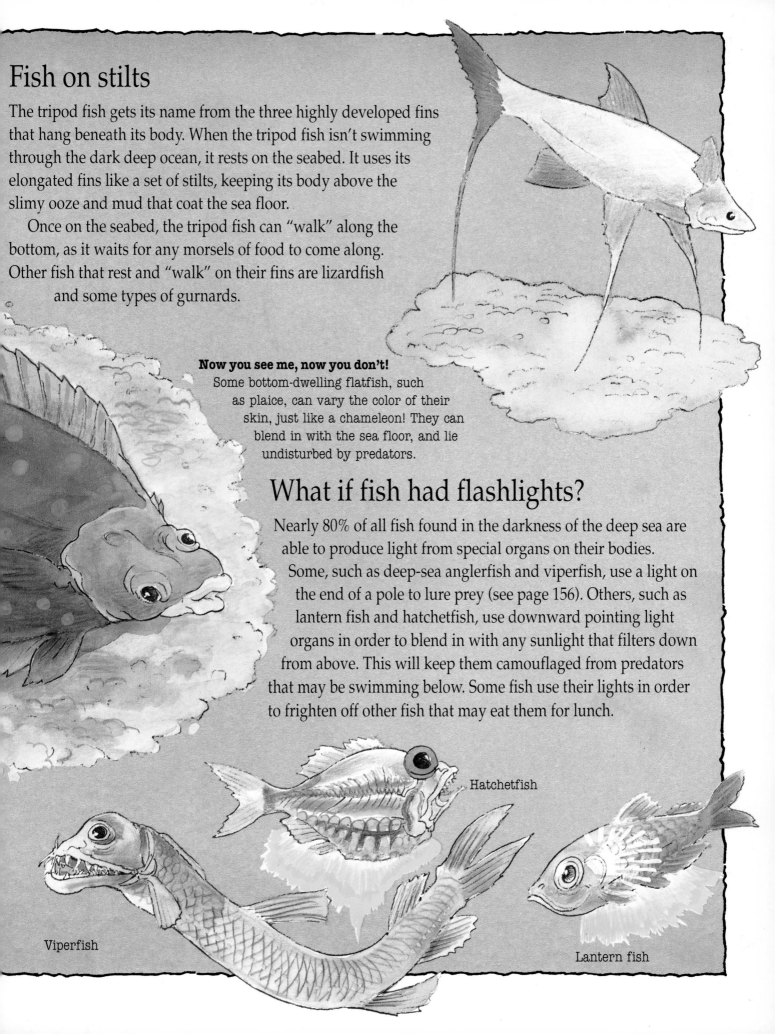

Hatchetfish

Viperfish

Lantern fish

WHAT IF THERE WERE NO MORE FISH?

In some lakes and rivers, and in some parts of the oceans, there are hardly any fish left. They have all been caught in nets or on lines, as food for people, pets, and farm animals; or they have been hooked by anglers for sport; or the water is so dirty and polluted that fish and other creatures cannot survive.

Many animals and plants rely on fish, whether it is the meat of their bodies or the nutrients from their decaying corpses. Either way, fish form a vital part of the watery ecosystem. If they were to disappear, as may happen in some parts of the world, the effects on the environment could be disastrous – many other species of animal could die out, too.

Global trash bin

Every day we humans dump thousands of tons of garbage, waste, and chemicals into the streams, rivers, and oceans of the world. But we hardly ever see the damage this causes.

We might notice an otter or a seabird on the surface, covered with oil from a ship that has illegally washed out its tanks. But we don't notice the thousands of fish suffocating and dying below the surface. The animal and plant life in many rivers and parts of the seas has been killed off by heavy pollution.

Birds
Dozens of seabird species, including albatrosses, cormorants, terns, pelicans, penguins, and many other birds, eat lots of fish. Without this source of food, they would starve.

Mammals

The many mammals that rely on fish to eat would probably become extinct. These include seals, dolphins, hunting whales, and otters.

What if fish were grown on farms?

Fish farming is carried out in many parts of the world. Trout, catfish, carp, and similar fish are grown in huge tanks or sealed lakes. They are fed and given clean, fresh water. Salmon and other saltwater fish are grown in huge wire-mesh cages suspended in the sea. They are also protected in these farms.

As a result, we have been able to provide a reliable source of fish. Before long we may be able to use fish farming to get all of our fish, without having to deplete natural fish stocks in the sea.

Invertebrates

Squid, octopuses, crabs, lobsters, jellyfish, anemones, and many other invertebrates (animals without backbones) hunt or catch a huge variety of fish to eat; or they might feed off their decaying bodies. Without fish, they may turn on each other for food.

Disappearing fish stocks

Modern fishing is big business, with modern fishing boats, using sonar equipment to find schools of fish, and enormous nets to catch them in. Every day these fleets of trawlers take vast quantities of fish from the sea.

However, the size of the fish and the number of fish taken has been decreasing in many parts of the oceans. In some places, such as the Grand Banks off the coast of Canada, fish have virtually disappeared. The fish cannot breed quickly enough to replace the numbers that humans catch.

GLOSSARY

Airfoil section
The special shape of an aircraft wing or propeller when seen edge-on, with the upper surface more curved than the lower surface. This gives a difference in air pressure and creates the force called *lift*.

Asteroid
A small, rocky body also known as a minor planet. In our solar system the greatest concentration of asteroids is in the asteroid belt between the planets Mars and Jupiter.

Atmosphere
Air, the mixture of gases around the Earth, which gradually thins out above heights of 60-120 miles into space. It has four main layers – the troposphere, stratosphere, mesosphere, and thermosphere.

Atoll
These are caused by corals growing on the sides of an oceanic volcano. The volcano, worn away by weather, slowly submerges and a ring of low-lying coral islands, or atolls, are left.

Biodiversity
The number of different species of plants or animals found in one area.

Black hole
A region in space that has a gravity so strong that nothing can escape from it.

Blubber
A thick layer of fat found in some sea mammals which helps to keep them warm in the cold sea.

Bony fish
A fish whose skeleton is made from bone.

Cartilaginous fish
A fish whose skeleton is made from cartilage.

Control surface
A panel on an aircraft that moves into the air flowing past, and helps to control the flight path.

Core
The innermost, middle, or central part of an object, such as the Earth. This is divided into the outer core – about 1,400 miles thick, and slightly flexible or "plastic," and an inner core – 1,700 miles across and solid.

Crust
The thin, hard outer layer which surrounds the Earth. Under the continents, the crust is 12-25 miles thick. Under the oceans it is much thinner, 3-7 miles thick.

Digestion
The breakdown and absorption of food into your body.

Diurnal
An animal that is awake during the day and sleeps at night.

Enzymes
Chemicals that increase the rate of a chemical change or reaction. In the case of digestion they break down large food particles to help the body absorb them.

Evolution
The changes that all living things have undergone in order to adapt to their environment over time.

Fin
Airplanes – the "tail," the upright part or vertical stabilizer, which is usually at the rear of an airplane. Sharks – the parts of the body that fish use to control their movement.

Fur
A coat of hair that covers many mammals and keeps them warm (and cool!).

Fuselage
The main "body" of a plane, which is usually a long, thin tube carrying the crew, passengers, and freight.

Galaxy
A huge group or cluster of stars separated from other galaxies by vast empty space. Our own galaxy is called the Galaxy or Milky Way.

Gills
The featherlike organs in some animals that absorb oxygen from the water as it flows over them.

Gravity
Gravitational force is the natural attracting force or pull exerted by all objects on all other objects. It is one of the four basic forces in the universe. The Sun's gravity keeps the Earth moving around it. The

Earth's gravity pulls us and all other objects down toward its center.

Hearing
The sense that allows you to pick up sounds using your ears.

Heart
The organ that pushes blood around the blood vessels.

Herd
A group of animals, ranging from a small family group to millions of different creatures.

Hibernation
The deep "sleep" that some creatures undergo during the winter months.

Lateral line
The line that runs down the length of the fish on either side. It is extremely sensitive and detects any vibrations in the water.

Lithosphere
The rigid outer shell of the Earth, about 60 miles deep. It includes the crust and the outer part of the mantle. It is divided jigsawlike into large lithospheric plates, whose slow movements cause continental drift.

Lungs
A pair of organs that are the sites of oxygen absorption.

Mach
A speed scale related to the speed of sound. Mach 1 is the speed of sound under given conditions such as pressure and temperature. This term is named after the Austrian scientist, Ernst Mach (1838-1916)

Magnetism
A force that can attract or repel objects containing iron. Electromagnetic force is one of the four basic forces in the universe.

Mantle
The thickest layer of the Earth under the outer crust, about 1,800 miles deep. Its rocks are hot and flow very slowly, creating the Earth's natural magnetic field.

Marsupial
Animals who give birth to very undeveloped young who then develop and grow inside the mother's pouch.

Meteor
Material from space that enters the Earth's atmosphere, glows with friction as it rushes through the air, and then burns up – a "shooting star." A meteorite is a meteor which has fallen to the Earth's surface.

Monotreme
A mammal that lays eggs instead of giving birth to live young.

Nocturnal
A creature that is asleep during the day and awake at night.

Orbit
The curved path of an object as it goes around a larger one. The Moon orbits the Earth, and the Earth orbits the Sun. Most orbits are oval shaped, called an *ellipse*.

Ozone Layer
A layer of atmosphere containing a form of normal oxygen gas – ozone. The ozone is mostly 10-28 miles above the earth, and is very thinly spread out compared to the other atmosphere gases. It helps to absorb harmful ultraviolet (UV) rays from the Sun, thereby protecting all living things.

Pitch
The angle of a plane when seen from

the side – that is whether it is pointing up – climbing, or down – diving.

Planet
A relatively large object that goes around a star, such as the nine planets orbiting the Sun.

Predator
An animal that actively hunts, kills, and eats other creatures.

Primate
The group of animals including monkeys, apes, and humans.

Pulse
The rate at which your heart beats.

Quasar
(Quasi-stellar object) A mysterious and extremely distant object that

GLOSSARY

shines like many galaxies, but which seems smaller in size than one galaxy. It may be a galaxy being born.

Red blood cells
The doughnut-shaped cell that gives blood its red color.

Respiration
The overall exchange of oxygen and carbon dioxide between lungs, blood, body cells, and the atmosphere.

Rotors
The long propeller-like blades on top of a helicopter, which provide lift

and also allow the helicopter to fly forward, backward, and sideways.

Ruminant
A plant-eating mammal with a four-chambered stomach, that is capable of regurgitating its food to chew again and so aid digestion.

Satellite
An object in space that orbits a larger object. So Earth is a satellite of the Sun, and the Moon is a satellite of the Earth. But the word "satellite" is usually used to mean an artificial or man-made space object.

Shoal
A group of fish that swim together. They can number up to several thousand. Also called a school.

Sight
The sense that lets you see the world around you using your eyes.

Skeleton
The structure that supports the body of a living organism.

Smell
The sense that allows you to experience odors, using smell cells in the roof of the nasal cavity.

Solar system
A group of planets that orbit a star. Our solar system has a total of nine planets that move around the Sun.

Spawn
When fish reproduce, it is called spawning.

Spiracle
An opening on an insect's skin that lets air into its breathing system.

Star
In astronomy, a star is an object that gives out energy as light, heat, and other forms of radiation.

STOL
Short Take-Off and Landing, meaning an aircraft that can go up or come down on a short runway. This can be a couple of hundred feet long.

Swim bladder
The spongy organ inside all bony fish which helps them to regulate the depth at which they swim.

Taste
The sense that lets you experience flavors, using taste buds on the tongue and upper throat.

Touch
The sense that allows you to feel the world around you. The majority of touch sensors are found in the skin.

Turbine
Set of fanlike angled blades used in machines such as power plant generators and aircraft engines.

Universe
All galaxies, stars, planets, as well as the space, cosmic dust, and all other matter between them.

Variable geometry
The proper name for a "swing-wing" plane, where the main wings usually swing straight out sideways for slow flight or takeoff, and sweep backward for fast flight.

Valve
A flaplike part of the blood system found in the heart and some veins. These close to stop blood from flowing the wrong way around the blood system.

White blood cell
These cells protect the body from foreign invaders, such as bacteria.

White dwarf
A small type or stage in the life of a star, possibly not much bigger than planets such as Jupiter. It is usually a star that is reaching the end of its life.

Yaw
The angle of a plane when seen from above or below – that is, whether it is flying straight ahead, or turning to the left or right.

INDEX